DUMB Goals

Your Leadership Blueprint for Mastering
the Art of Turning Vision into Extraordinary
Action

Julie Jamison

QUANTUM SHIFT
PUBLISHING

For information about special discounts for bulk purchases, please contact julie@thejuliejamison.com.

Editing, Interior, and Cover Design by Quantum Shift Media.

ISBN 978-1-955533-34-8 (print)
ISBN 978-1-955533-35-5 (hardback)
ISBN 978-1-955533-36-2 (eBook)
Library of Congress Control Number: 2024919960

Printed in the United States

QUANTUM SHIFT
P U B L I S H I N G

Port St. Lucie, Florida

DEDICATION

To my husband, Joe, the love of my life, my arm candy, and my greatest supporter:

I dedicate this book to you for holding on to the reins of life with me through every twist and turn and for always encouraging me to go higher, reach further, and dream bigger.

Your unwavering support, belief in me, and love for me have been the foundation of every success and the strength behind every challenge I've faced.

Thank you for being my partner, cheerleader, and greatest love.

This journey wouldn't have been possible without you.

With all my love,

Julie

PREFACE

Have you ever had a dream so big, so bold, that it scared you? A dream that seemed impossible, something others might laugh at or dismiss as pure fantasy?

I have. And that's precisely the dream you need to chase.

Welcome to *DUMB Goals*, where we turn the impossible into the inevitable. This book isn't about playing it safe or setting goals you're comfortable with. It's about pushing boundaries, shattering expectations, and daring to dream bigger than you ever thought possible.

I grew up in Parma, Ohio, a suburb of Cleveland, surrounded by a family steeped in the automotive and manufacturing industries. From an early age, I learned to work hard, trust my instincts, and set clear, attainable goals that would take me further than the generation before. But I also had a burning passion for creating—whether it was sketching, painting, designing ball gowns, or envisioning grand mansions. My love for art was insatiable, and it followed me even as I entered the technical world of aviation, nuclear operations, and leadership, where I served nearly 13 years in the U.S. Air Force.

From the outside, my journey might seem like a series of illogical steps—military service, corporate leadership, and eventually starting my luxury fine art galleries. But what drove me at every turn wasn't logic. It was a large vision that terrified and excited me to dream so big that those around me looked at me like I had a third eyeball. I believed I could blend the traditional with the futuristic and create art that captivated people and stood the test of time as a valuable investment. It was the belief that my "delusional" goals weren't just daydreams—they were the blueprint for my daily steps to further success.

By delusional, I mean the type of goal that makes everyone around you feel that you have mentally lost your marbles. The kind that only one person you trust in your life may understand. The one you call and say, "I need to run something by you. I have an idea," and they respond by building upon the idea.

This book is more than just my story; it's a guide for anyone who has ever dared to dream big. *DUMB Goals* will challenge you to think differently, get comfortable being outside your comfort zone, and question the limits you and lifelong programming have placed on you. Through the principles of

DUMB Goals (Delusional, Uncomfortable, Move Out, and Blocks), I'll show you how to transform those wild, crazy dreams into tangible reality.

But let's be clear—this isn't a journey for the faint of heart. My book may offend some. But for those who know they were meant to follow their dreams and create a life they have always known they are supposed to live, this is the book for you to take your life to the level you always dreamed of. This book is for dreamers, doers, and visionaries who refuse to settle for anything less than extraordinary. It's for those ready to take that first step, no matter how scary it might seem, and to keep going even when the path is anything but straightforward.

As you turn these pages, I want you to feel the same fire that fueled my journey. I want you to see that every challenge or setback is another opportunity to rise above. This book is your companion on a journey of growth, learning, and the relentless pursuit of your dreams and purpose.

You don't need anyone's permission or validation to dream big. All you need is the courage to take that first step and the determination to keep going, no matter what. Together, we'll explore what it means to set goals that others might call delusional—and why those are the only goals worth pursuing.

So, here's to the dreamers, the risk-takers, the ones who refuse to play it safe. Let's make those delusional dreams a reality. Because with the right mindset, nothing is impossible.

ACKNOWLEDGMENTS

My Babies

To my dearest Ava, Joseph, Lily, and James— thank you for giving me the most incredible gift of all: the privilege of being your mom. Each day with you is filled with love, laughter, and lessons I cherish deeply. You are my inspiration, and my desire to create a world where your dreams can flourish fuels every step I take. Your dad and I work hard to pave the way for you to be the movers and shakers I know you are destined to become.

Your energy, curiosity, and determination remind me daily of your limitless potential. My hope is that you see how deeply I believe in each of you and that this belief empowers you to chase after your passions with confidence and courage.

Always remember, I love you beyond measure, and my pride in you is unwavering—no matter what. Go out there and change the world, not by being anyone other than your amazing, authentic selves. The world needs your light, and I am endlessly proud to witness the impact you will undoubtedly make.

Parents and Family

To my parents, sister, and family, thank you for teaching me the value of caution and thoughtfulness, while encouraging me to be unapologetically myself. Your guidance has allowed me to balance wisdom with boldness, giving me the confidence to embrace who I am as I navigate life's challenges. I am deeply grateful for your love and support—it has shaped me into who I am today.

Girlfriends and Leaders

To my incredible girlfriends and fellow leaders, you quickly recognized that I'm a thinker, doer, and mover, and your unwavering support has been invaluable. Thank you for standing by, challenging, and inspiring me to keep pushing forward. Your belief in me and fierce determination fuel my drive, and I am grateful to share this journey with such powerful, visionary women.

Editor & Publisher

A heartfelt thank you to my editor, Keren Kilgore, and Quantum Shift Media for jumping on board with my delusional goal-setting train. Your support in honing my message while keeping it authentic has been invaluable. Without your hard work and dedication, I couldn't have produced and published this book as efficiently.

WORKBOOK

Download the Workbook that accompanies this book to implement the exercises to accomplish your DUMB Goals. It will guide you through the process of putting your goals into action.

thejuliejamison.com/DUMBGoalsWorkbook

CONTENTS

CHAPTER 1

What Are DUMB Goals?

What Are DUMB Goals?

The Power of DUMB Goals

In a world that often emphasizes practicality and risk aversion, the concept of DUMB goals stands out as a radical approach to goal setting. These goals aren't just about setting targets but transforming your mindset beyond metrics, your approach to challenges, and your life. This book is for entrepreneurs, military leaders, athletes, and all dreamers who refuse to settle for the ordinary—individuals ready to take action and get closer and closer to their target.

DUMB goals represent a framework for those who dare to dream bigger, push harder, and achieve what others deem impossible. The acronym stands for:

- **Delusional**

  Setting delusional goals means pursuing objectives that seem wildly unrealistic or unattainable, challenging conventional boundaries of what's possible. This approach pushes you to unlock additional levels of creativity and drive, leading to potentially groundbreaking achievements.

- **Uncomfortable**

  Setting delusional goals requires getting comfortable with being uncomfortable, as these objectives push you far beyond your comfort zone. Embracing this discomfort is essential, as it drives growth and innovation, enabling you to achieve what once seemed impossible.

- **Move Out**

  In the military, "move out" signifies the moment to take decisive action, a critical mindset in delusional goal setting. Overthinking can stall progress; pursuing ambitious goals requires you to overcome analysis paralysis and take bold, immediate action toward your vision, trusting your instincts and adaptability.

- **Blocks**

  In delusional goal setting, removing "blocks" is crucial, particularly the mental "neuro blocks" you unconsciously place in your path. These self-imposed barriers can stifle progress and keep you from achieving your most ambitious goals. Identifying and dismantling them to move forward with confidence and clarity is essential.

Each component encourages you to set goals that challenge you to break through your conventional thinking, push beyond perceived limitations, take actionable steps, and remove the mental barriers that often hinder success.

My Story

Ever since I was a child, I've been a dreamer. I remember hours spent drawing visions of gowns, mansions, and fantastical worlds in my sketchbook. My imagination knew no bounds, and the adults around me often encouraged my creativity by saying, "You can be anything you want to be!" or "You have some amazing interests."

Growing up in America in the late 1980s to the early 2000s, society and my parents taught me that success meant attending college and getting a job. As the youngest of two girls, this felt like a daunting goal, especially for someone who hated school. When I graduated kindergarten, my mother asked me, "Julie, are you excited to go to 1st grade?" My six-year-old sarcastic and no-fear self replied, "I'm not going back to school; I've already learned!" That's a famous quote in our family to this day.

Later, as I was preparing to graduate high school, I was told that to be successful in college, I must choose a degree that would put food on the table for my family. To this day, when choosing a degree, you must have a return on your investment if you spend over six figures on a really expensive piece of paper and a box checked for a job interview. Don't get me wrong, I have multiple degrees from which I learned a boatload, but they were technical degrees in aviation. Yes, we should have educated pilots with years of experience before allowing them to put people's lives in their hands. I also use my degree to teach aerodynamics and hypoxia to my two older children. You see, I love, and I mean love, to learn, but the school assignments are what I believe took my joy in learning to a dreaded task.

When I decided to study aviation in college, it was on a whim. I initially looked at Kent State University's Architecture program, then saw airplanes and thought, *Those look cool. I should do that!* I have my private pilot license but have been unable to fly for years because of work and four children. It is the most freeing experience to take off for your first solo flight. I'm not crazy about heights, but I am not jumping out of the plane and have complete control!

While attending Kent State University in Kent, Ohio, I simultaneously started the Air Force Reserve Officer Training Corps, AFROTC or ROTC. I remember having a conversation with my parents, specifically with my mom, about how I did not want to go to college. I felt so burned out from the college prep high school environment, I did not want to continue school. With a long line of very skilled mechanics, electricians, and woodworkers in the family, my parents talked about trade school.

To help decide which college and career path to follow, our high school gave us the opportunity to shadow a career field we were interested in for three days. Well, when you are the parent of a child who is interested in everything, what do you do? My Mom magically set up three career fields to shadow: Air Traffic Control, Physical Therapy, and Air Force Recruiter.

My interest in Air Traffic Control came from a History Channel TV show I watched with my dad every weekend called "Dog Fights." I was obsessed with learning about history from ancient Egypt to World War II.

My interest in Physical Therapy came from my nearly 16 years of dancing, even though my hips were designed for childbearing, not Swan Lake. However, this never stopped me from doing what I loved.

Three things influenced my interest in the military: watching the Disney movie *Mulan,* learning about WWII and wearing uniforms for 13 years in Catholic school, and wanting to serve after 9/11. I always wanted to be part of something bigger.

How does this all relate to goal setting? I set goals and then make them my reality. When I joined AFROTC, I was a girly girl with impeccable hair and makeup perfected from years of dance performances; no one could touch my neat hair and makeup. I was also the one that a friend and peer of mine stated about three years into the program, "Jamison, I didn't think you would last two weeks!" I remember smiling and saying, "Well, I guess I outlasted the others." He and I knew we started with about 40 cadets in freshman year. This conversation occurred in the spring semester of our junior year, during which we had about ten still standing. By the time we were commissioned as officers into the active-duty United States Air Force, we were down to about seven from the original group. So yes, my stubbornness and drive have served me well.

I am not the best of test takers, but I am stubborn and driven. I fought to stay in the program, and if it were not for our amazing mentors, leaders, and instructors, I would not have remained on the path to becoming a United States Air Force Officer.

There is a test called the AFOQT, the Air Force Officer Qualifications Test. It is like the ACT and SAT tests on steroids. The test had multiple sections, from math to verbal skills and a pilot portion. The part that became my nemesis was the verbal section. When I took the test, I was unaware of the minimum required to pass. Well, reading fast is not my strong suit; numbers and spatial awareness are where I thrive.

Long story short, I failed! No big deal. This is life; I have failed before. However, I did not understand that passing this test was mandatory to become a commissioned officer. So, I waited for approximately six months to retest. I did, and then I failed again! Yes, I prepared with every book available, but my techniques did not work well because I did worse on the second test.

I could only test again with a waiver from the Air Force gods. Fortunately, when I was devastated and broken down, I had leadership who saw my potential. This time, my study approach shifted quite a bit. As I called my parents, crying my eyes out, they said well, let's see what our options are. They understood that hiring the right team was vital to success. So, they gave me the gift of tutoring, and I started preparing to test a third time, even though the waiver process would take months.

One day, my commander called and said I was approved to test for a third time. Panic immediately ensued because it was performance time. As a 20-year-old, I did not want to disappoint anyone who supported me through this process. Remember when I said I highly disliked school? Although I performed well in school, receiving As and Bs and sometimes a C (most likely in English), my efforts took longer than others. If a standard student studied for one hour, I studied three because it just took longer, especially in subjects I did not enjoy.

Fortunately, after hours of testing and waiting for test results for a few weeks, my instructors called to let me know I had passed! But this was only to get me to field training, known as the AFROTC boot camp, midway through the program. Why two years through the program? This allows time for the instructors and commander to assess if the cadet is serious about being an officer and leader in the U.S. Air Force, pass basic medical requirements, pass your AFOQT, and assess your basic followership and leadership skills. The cadet must earn their ticket to field training and commissioning. During the 2008 – 2011 recession, we were told you were not guaranteed a commission because we were downsizing our forces. Well, if this is not a fire under your ass, I do not know what is.

Finally, after much effort, I made it to the week of commissioning during senior year spring semester finals. Three days before our commissioning ceremony, I found out I was no longer approved for my career field because I failed the depth perception on the eye exam during my flight physical. I learned years later that this is a simple test to fail when your eyes are dehydrated or tired. However, they were fine to earn my private pilot's license and passed all the FAA requirements. I know everything happens for a reason, and I always end up where I am supposed to be when I am supposed to be there. So, when I received a follow-up phone call from my Senior NCO (Non-commissioned Officer), stating that I needed to build a new "Dream Sheet" and be in her office at 8:00 AM the next day, I did not know what to feel.

A dream sheet is part of the recruiting process to list up to six career fields you would be interested in doing as your full-time job in the military. For AFROTC Cadets, this process occurs once they successfully pass their field training between junior year and submit their dream sheet in the spring semester of junior year. I could not tell you exactly what I put on my dream sheet, but my selections were primarily aviation related. Many people think that when they join the military, especially the Air Force, they are going to be a fighter pilot or special ops. However, pilots alone are less than 4% of Air Force Officers. Career fields are based on the needs of the military at the time you signed up to serve.

Learning this was a very humbling experience for me. When I met with the NCO the next morning, my new Dream Sheet had: Intelligence Officer, Aircraft Maintenance Officer, and more. Nothing on my list was available. I remember being in my NCO's office, and she said Space and Missiles are only available. My dream sheet was not even considered.

Space and Missiles was a career field I knew nothing about. However, God was orchestrating a plan. As I sat with the NCO, I now say I was hand selected to be a Nuclear Missile Operator.

As an ignorant 22-year-old, I did not know we still had Intercontinental Ballistic Missiles. I am pretty sure when my leadership explained what the career field was, I stated something like, "We still have those?" I thought we had gotten rid of them after the Cold War. But once I got into the mission, I understood the importance of this and being the incognito out of the news career field.

Although we had a very low retainability rate, within the career field, I met some amazing friends, and if it were not for those around me, it would have been difficult to succeed in the high-tempo, high-stress industry. With 24-hour shifts, we called Alert and were ready to launch a missile at a moment's notice, 24/7, 365. Some of us nicknamed it "death and bunny slippers." The goal was to deter our adversaries from ever needing to use these extremely powerful weapons of mass destruction.

Moving forward in my career, I had the opportunity to become an instructor approximately one year after being a Deputy Missile Combat Crew Operator. Throughout my nearly five years at my missile base in Cheyenne, Wyoming, I became an instructor and evaluator multiple times before moving to my next duty location. These were some of the most rewarding roles. I learned so much and could provide explanations when peers and students asked about the "why" behind how the mechanics of the missile function. Some of my best, more senior instructors showed me through their actions that you don't know everything, so always do your research and never shoot from the hip. If you don't know something, look it up so you understand it well enough to teach it in different ways.

After the missile field from 2016 to 2019, I became an action officer advising our military senior leaders about the missile field operations. This was an amazing learning opportunity as a midlevel Captain. I understood the strategic vision of our senior leaders while being a fly on the wall and learning. I encourage any rank to take on these roles to learn how our policies, regulations, and strategic operations are planned by those with decades more experience than ourselves.

Next, in 2019, I served as an alumnus at Kent State University, where my years of instructing and evaluating led me to become a Master Instructor before departing Air Force ROTC for the Air Force Reserve and corporate leadership. It was always a dream of mine when the planets aligned to come back and teach to give back and support the future Air Force officers who may need someone to believe in them, just as my instructors believed in me.

Family

My husband Joe and I met through the AFROTC program. As a freshman, I was too worried to look around while standing at attention, so I had no idea he stood beside me. We randomly started talking in the spring semester of my junior year after he was out of the program. On our first date, we went to the shooting range and then out for Italian food. It was love! We were married at the end of my senior year in college, and well, the rest is history.

Joe inspired me to be the best version of myself. He was smart, driven, and protective, and we always encouraged each other to be better and dream bigger. Joe also makes me laugh, which is very important in a relationship.

We were young and in love and took the leap of faith to get engaged after only four months. When I took Joe to meet my parents and have dinner before getting engaged, my dad talked to Joe the entire evening. My dad had never talked to any of my previous boyfriends. I knew then he was a keeper. We were married at the end of my senior year, less than a year after being engaged, and entered the active-duty Air Force a few months later.

When Joe and I dated, we discussed having two children. If we didn't have a boy, we'd have three kids. We had our two oldest children, now nearly 11 (daughter) and 9 (son), while stationed in Wyoming.

After finally being out of the diaper phase, we were completely content but threw a grenade in the mix and added two more children. When we planned for our third child, a global pandemic was not on our baby checklist. Our now 4-year-old daughter was born at the beginning of COVID at the beginning of 2020 after making our way back to Ohio. And, we thought, if you have three children, why not round it out to four? All four of my children have completely distinct personalities, which means my husband and I must be four different versions of parents.

My daughter, Ava, came first; she has been the leader of the pack, smart, driven, creative, and gorgeous. She always talks like mom, even when I remind her she is not. Ava will accomplish anything she sets her mind to. I love that she wants to try everything in life, from dance to karate to art. She will be a force in any goal she has in life. I love that she speaks her mind and knows she is destined to live life to the fullest.

Next came Joseph. They say the first son is the male version of mom. He sounds like me when I was a child and is extremely creative, drawing and imagining what he wants out of life. I can see him designing buildings, as he talks about building castles with secret tunnels and some amazing designs. I love that Joseph is strong, driven, and creative.

Now my post COVID babies came while instructing AFROTC at Kent State University. My younger daughter Lily came next, and she was planned prior to COVID and arrived at the height of staying at home in the spring of 2020. This child has zero fear and runs headfirst at life. She also believes she is the mom of the house and thinks she can do whatever she wants. She often tells us, "No, it's OK, I'm allowed." Lily loves to go fast with her blonde curls flowing in the wind. I love her free spirit.

My youngest, James, was born just before leaving Air Force active duty and heading to corporate in 2022. He is 100% a mama's boy. Extremely smart, he picks up skills faster than his older siblings and often outsmarts us all. I love that he always wants to help and insists upon it. If mom and dad are not sitting down, he will not sit and relax. He, too, runs headfirst at life, but sometimes so fast he hurts himself.

All my children keep me grounded and humble, which has supported me in my career. Whenever you need honest feedback, your children will give it to you for free without asking. They have a very clear vision of seeing through bullshit, and they always let me know. My children have made me a better leader. They made me even more empathetic and patient than I thought I ever could be.

They especially support my DUMB goals! Sometimes when I have an idea, the first person I tell is one of my children. They brainstorm with me and build upon my ideas. They say, "Yeah!" then ask, "What else could we do to make this even better?" For example, brainstorming ideas about my company, they would come into my and say, "I have an idea for your art," or "I think you should have an in-person place for your art." I would often build upon their advice or feedback for tweaks to make my work better.

After starting my galleries, my oldest two children have come to me with so many ideas of what they want to do with their lives. I believe this goes back to what we tell them: "That is a great idea; you should go do that." They do not let the problems of the world interfere with the ideas flowing through them. They are a safe place to brainstorm and vet many of my DUMB goals, create amazing conversations, and allow our creativity to partner and work together.

From my years in Air Force leadership, joining the corporate forces, and taking the leap of faith in myself to create my galleries, I knew it was time to help think bigger, no matter the size of the goal. Small or large, by the end of our DUMB goals journey, I will have you saying, "Let's make the goal even bigger!"

The Evolution of Goal Setting

Goal setting isn't just a task—it's the heartbeat of personal and professional growth. But let's be honest: The way we've been taught to set goals is limited for entrepreneurs and innovators. Sure, traditional methods like SMART goals—Specific, Measurable, Achievable, Relevant, and Time-bound—have their place. They were the bedrock of my early career, guiding me with structure and discipline when I needed it most.

Without SMART goals, I wouldn't have had the roadmap to reach those initial milestones. They gave me the confidence to conquer each step, one after the other, and build a solid foundation. Every time I checked off a SMART goal, it was like adding another brick to the fortress of my success. But as I matured in my career and leadership, something became very clear: the higher I climbed, the more these SMART goals felt like a ceiling instead of a launchpad.

SMART goals are safe. They're realistic. But let's face it—realistic doesn't bring an extraordinary vision into the world. There came a point when playing it safe wouldn't cut it anymore. I needed to break free from the incremental, the ordinary and aim for something that would blow the roof off my potential.

This is where evolution began. I knew I couldn't abandon the structure that had gotten me this far, but I also knew that to achieve truly extraordinary outcomes, I had to think bigger. Much bigger. That's when I shifted from SMART goals to DUMB goals—a framework designed to defy limits, challenge the status quo, and inspire visionary ambition.

DUMB goals aren't for the faint of heart. They demand you to dream so big it feels uncomfortable, to aim for the impossible, and to push past what anyone—including yourself—might think attainable. This isn't just goal setting; this is life-altering, boundary-breaking, no-holds-barred ambition.

The shift from SMART to DUMB Goals isn't just about aiming higher; it's about recognizing that innovation and risk-taking are not optional in a constantly changing world—it's vital to lean into the risk. As we journey through this book, you'll discover how DUMB goals can transform your approach to life and work, especially in environments where adaptability and boldness are the keys to success.

So, buckle up, because this is where the real fun begins. The days of playing it safe are over. It's time to set goals that will make you—and everyone around you—stop in their tracks. Welcome to the world of *DUMB Goals*. Let's get started!

CHAPTER 2

Delusional Thinking

Delusional Thinking

So, let's dive right in and set your DUMB goals. When setting goals, don't just think big—think DUMB: Delusional, Uncomfortable, Move Out, and Blocks. Being delusional doesn't mean you've lost touch with reality; it means letting your creativity flow without limits as you write your goals. Whether on a napkin, a designated notebook, or any format that resonates with you, writing them down is the first step. You're not just setting goals; you're creating the reality you want to live in today. It's about carving in stone what you genuinely want out of life, and that's the key to your success. Later, in Chapter 6, we'll dive deeper into exercises to help you refine this process, but for now, start by asking yourself, "What do I truly want in life?"

What Do You Believe You Want?

It seems simple, right? But you'd be surprised how many people have no idea what they really want and believe they can have in life. Oprah Winfrey once said, "You don't become what you want, you become what you believe."[1] Notice that this statement does not blame others for your reality;

it is taking ownership of your reality. It's not only about wanting something; it's about believing deep down that you can achieve it. This belief drives your actions, decisions, and, ultimately, your success. Goal setting is much the same; if you're unclear or don't believe in your capacity to achieve, even the clearest goals can remain out of reach. This isn't about a spiritual journey—though it can be if you believe in something greater than yourself—but about looking inward and recognizing your immense power to create the life you believe is possible.

When I started GATE 28 & J. Rose Scrolls By Julie Jamison Galleries, I had to consider what I wanted or believe I wanted out of my business. My initial business goals were straightforward: do something I enjoy, wear stretchy pants, and take and pick up my kids from school. What I found is I did not set the "why" behind my goal right away. Why do I want to do something I enjoy? Because I want to own my schedule. Why do I want to own my schedule? Because I do not want those around me to control my time, and I want to own my time. Why do you want to own my time? Because time is the only resource in life that I cannot replenish. Why do you feel you cannot replenish your time? Because Covid-19 taught me life is short, I want to take advantage of the time I may or may not have, spend it with those I love, and experience the joys in life. Why do you want to take advantage of your time? Because time equals true freedom.

Prior to leaving my corporate leadership role as a quality manager in manufacturing, I had the opportunity to complete what is called "Better Up" Coaching, which offered amazing support from executive leadership to communication skills and more. It was this building on my years of military leadership training that taught me a beautiful word, *No*. I was unaware that setting a boundary in my time was everything. I remember describing my "work-life balance" and the number of tasks on my plate as a "turkey platter" that could hold more tasks. Learning to say *no* was not something I was taught to do in my leadership or personal life. I was taught to help everyone and find a way to say *yes*. What I discovered quickly is that self-care is not selfish. Resting is required for all of us, even wives, moms, and leaders.

Unfortunately, when you allow yourself to be a perfectionist and workaholic, like me, you tell those around you, including your team, peers, and boss, that this is the level of performance you plan to maintain forever. Having the reality check to say *no* to short time-sucking tasks that do not help the company, your team, or yourself grow is essential. I found myself working 14- to 16-hour days, not seeing my family, not sleeping, and feeling burned out because I could not learn to respect my time.

Why is this relevant to goal setting?

This ties back to delusional goal setting because when you're aiming for goals that seem impossible to others—goals that push the limits of what's expected—you must be fiercely protective of your time and energy. Knowing your "why" behind each goal gives you the clarity to say *no* to distractions and lesser priorities so you can say *yes* to the actions that truly move the needle. For me, saying *no* was essential to staying focused on my ultimate vision of building the family empire and not missing out on life. Delusional-level goals require unwavering commitment, and that only happens when you're rooted in your deeper purpose and willing to let go of anything that doesn't align with it.

Corporate to Fine Art Galleries

After leaving my quality manager role, I didn't immediately start my company. Instead, I applied for similar positions in manufacturing, driven by my ingrained safety habits. I was frequently asked about my enthusiasm for creating and building improved operations during multiple interviews. I was excited when a company invited me back for further discussions, as they seemed genuinely interested in enhancing quality across their shop floor. However, as we toured the facility, I realized they were significantly behind the environment I had previously left, with a much smaller team to address the needed improvements. While this initially thrilled me because it seemed like an opportunity to make a meaningful impact and be creative with the team, I soon recognized that I would likely end up repeating the same cycle, whether in a quality or operations manager role. Having experienced burnout, I started discussing options with my husband and how I felt I needed to work for myself. I had brought this up with my Better Up coach months prior and stated I would plan to start my company in maybe three to five years. I was not sure what that company would be, but I knew I was tired and wanted to own my time. I realized my choosing not to return to the corporate world was the way to go for the sake of health and happiness. My husband, Joe, said his chest hurt for three weeks thinking about the enormous risk I was taking as we both brought in good paychecks to support our four children. Once we started learning more about the benefits of owning a business, we were on the same page, and to this day, we brainstorm and grow the galleries together.

As I entertained the idea of starting my company, I followed multiple social media influencers on how to accomplish affiliate marketing. I chose to invest in a class, which was beneficial, but I wanted to own the product that I was selling. I started designing journals, phone cases, and more. Then, I took another course in marketing and online coaching. This was also beneficial as I was learning what my niche was.

I found a few months in that I needed to narrow my offers and sell them well. My designs for journals to phone cases were very good, but business was not going where I wanted it to, and the purpose felt disconnected. Telling your parents after years of degrees you are choosing to leave a stable paycheck for making journals was not a fun discussion. There was a lot of fear about how Joe and I would continue to maintain our lifestyle with four children. I remember asking them, "When have I ever set my mind to something and not accomplished it?" We could not come up with one situation in my life where my determined mind allowed me to fail.

I faced doubts from all angles. This is why successful people tell you not to discuss your ideas with people close to you, especially family. My family knew me as the girl who was always dreaming up big ideas, but they weren't sure if those dreams could translate into real-world success. It's not that they didn't believe in me; it's that the same societal norms had conditioned them. They believed in safety, security, and the steady paycheck from a traditional career path.

After leaving the corporate office life, I began hiking five days a week, during "business hours" after taking my children to school and daycare. I felt I was getting away with something, being away from my desk during the day, being able to let my children to and from school, and not being worried about receiving work calls. While on my hikes, I took photos every day of the gorgeous fall and winter landscapes. This is when my creativity took off to a different level. "I will sell fine art... But how?" I remember running this idea by Joe, and he naturally was concerned about how I would sell my work. I remember saying the famous quote from *The Field of Dreams*, "you build it they will come."

In the 21st century, now that we have the internet, you can learn almost anything from video tutorials. I invested in a professional Nikon Z8 camera and lenses and started learning the new equipment. I quickly realized my professional camera was much different from taking photographs on my phone or a small digital camera. My photographs were terrible! I started taking my camera on every hike to learn its true capability. This allowed me to practice most days of the week until it became a natural extension of me. I could see the photograph before it was taken and knew roughly how I would edit it. To this day, I believe I can always improve and be better at my craft, and I will continue to do so throughout my career.

This time was exciting, and I finally felt like I had found my true niche. But stepping out of this comfort zone required more than just a change in thinking—it required a change in belief. The first step was to recognize that the constraints of my previous roles did not limit my potential. I had to believe that I was capable of much more than what I had been doing, that I could create something entirely new, something the world has never seen. Fine Art is not just a good investment; it's very presence is a safe place to calm the many stressors in life. I did not build a need; I built a want. I create exclusive 1 of 1 Fine Art Photography, where only 28 prints are released each month. I create beautiful landscapes, architecture, and floral pieces that clients worldwide appreciate the exclusivity of being the only one with that piece.

This business model is uncommon in the world of fine art photography. There are only one or two other artists who release 1 of 1 photography. This is where DUMB goals officially began.

The Evolution from SMART to DUMB Goals

This evolution from SMART goals to DUMB goals wasn't just a shift in thinking but a shift in beliefs. SMART goals served me well in the past. They gave me structure and discipline and helped me achieve incremental success. But they would never help me achieve the extraordinary. I needed something more. I needed to think in terms of DUMB goals—Delusional, Uncomfortable, Move Out, and Blocks.

DUMB goals are the goals that make people look at you like you've lost your mind. They are goals that seem so far beyond the realm of possibility that they defy logic and reason. But these goals will push you to your limits and beyond, forcing you to grow, adapt, and innovate in ways you never thought possible.

When I first started thinking about my DUMB goals, I realized they were all about creating something that didn't exist yet—something that would combine my love of art with my desire to make a positive impact on the world. I wanted to create a gallery that wasn't just a place to showcase art but a place where art could be used as a tool for change. I wanted to create a space where artists and collectors could unite to support causes that mattered and where art could raise awareness and fund important issues.

For example, by leading my company with service first, it was important to me to give back to our community. This is why I chose to support children by giving 10% of all net profits to The Boys and Girls Club of America. My husband and I started giving back with small donations on behalf of the company before sales began to come in on a regular basis because we believe it is important to lead with your cause first, and the rest falls into place. This, to me, was what fed my personal core values of people, service, and integrity.

Visionary Thinking—The Heart of DUMB Goals

At the heart of DUMB goals is visionary thinking— the ability to imagine a future that is radically different and better than the present. Visionary thinking drives innovation and progress. It allows individuals and organizations to break new ground, challenge the status quo, and achieve what was once thought impossible. Take, for instance, the Wright brothers' first flight, the moon landing, or the development of the internet—each monumental achievement began with someone daring to think beyond what was possible at the time.

But creating this kind of space required more than just a vision. Vision is the ability to see beyond your current circumstances, to imagine a future that doesn't yet exist, and to set your sights on ambitious, even delusional, goals that push you out of your comfort zone. It's about clarity and direction—a mental picture of what you want to achieve. However, vision alone isn't enough.

It required belief—the deep, unshakable confidence that I could make it happen, that my vision had value, and that there was a market for it. Belief is the fuel that transforms vision into action. It's what drives you to keep pushing forward, even when the world around you might say it's impossible. I had to believe in my vision so strongly that it became a reality in my mind long before it existed in the physical world. As *Napoleon Hill* famously stated in his book *Think and Grow Rich*, "Whatever the mind can conceive and believe, it can achieve."[2]

Vision without belief is just a dream. But when you pair a clear, compelling vision with an unwavering belief in its success, you create a powerful force for action. This belief shapes your mindset, decisions, and daily habits, aligning them with your goals until your vision becomes tangible.

For me, visionary thinking started young. As a child, I constantly designed mansions and luxury-style homes in my mind and in sketches. I visualized every detail—the layout, the smells, the colors. Playing with my toys wasn't about the dolls but about laying out my Barbie house with a flow that made sense. Even then, I was using visionary thinking to create spaces that felt real and tangible long before I knew the power of this mindset.

This kind of creative visualization is at the core of DUMB goals. It's about seeing the world not just as it is but as it could be—transforming the abstract into something tangible, believing in your vision even if only in your mind at first.

As I got older, I began to see that this thinking wasn't just useful for designing Barbie houses—it was helpful in designing my life. When I started my company, I used the same creative visualization to imagine what it could and would be. I pictured the online gallery spaces as a worldwide way to reach collectors who love fine art and photography. I visualized the fine art shows and fairs I would have with my art hanging on the walls as wildly successful. I saw myself talking with collectors, art dealers, luxury interior designers, and four- and five-star hotel owners selecting the perfect piece for their environment. The more I saw the details, the more it became my reality.

That's the power of visionary thinking—it allows you to create the reality you want starting from the inside out. Visionary thinking isn't just about dreaming big; it's about believing so strongly in your vision that you bring it to life through your actions.

When Elon Musk announced his goal to colonize Mars, many thought it was impossible, if not delusional. Yet his visionary thinking drove SpaceX to achieve unprecedented milestones, including the first privately funded spacecraft to reach the International Space Station. Though often deemed outlandish, this kind of thinking can lead to groundbreaking achievements that redefine what's possible.

The same applies to you—by setting DUMB goals, you challenge yourself to dream big, think creatively, and push through challenges.

Encouraging Delusional Thinking in Children

It's ironic that we encourage young children to think big and dream of becoming astronauts, artists, or even superheroes, but as they grow older, we often start to limit their aspirations. We tell them to be realistic, to choose a practical career path, and always have a Plan B if things go wrong. In doing so, we unintentionally quash their creative problem-solving abilities and their willingness to think outside the box.

Tony Robbins discusses the importance of maintaining a childlike sense of wonder and possibility. He argues that this mindset allows people to achieve extraordinary things. Children naturally embrace delusional thinking—they don't see the world in terms of limitations but in endless possibilities.

As adults, we can learn a lot from this mindset. Instead of telling children to be realistic, we should encourage them to explore their wildest dreams.

We should nurture their creativity and help them develop the skills to make those dreams a reality. By fostering a culture of delusional thinking from a young age, we can raise a generation of innovators, leaders, and change-makers who aren't afraid to push the boundaries of what's possible.

Today, there are times when I discuss my dreams for my company with my two older children. What I love about these conversations is that my nearly 11-year-old daughter Ava and 9-year-old son Joseph don't shut down the ideas; they build on them. For example, when I talked with them about wanting to build a mansion for our family, they excitedly contributed with suggestions like, "We could have stained glass windows!" and "Let's include secret tunnels to get around!" Children don't see limits—they only see possibilities. Their energy and enthusiasm are infectious, and together, we created a bigger and bolder vision than anything I could have imagined on my own.

This kind of creative collaboration is a perfect example of how delusional thinking can be cultivated and expanded upon. Children naturally think this way, and when we encourage it, we create an environment where ideas can grow and flourish. It's a reminder that we, too, should embrace and feed our 5-year-old self with this mindset in our lives, work, and purpose.

Applying Delusional Thinking in Real Life

So now you may ask, "Okay, great, Julie, but how in the world do I do this?" The answer lies in a simple yet powerful principle: Step 1—Never ask "How?" Always ask yourself, "What is my next step?"

As a Type A, outcome-driven individual, it took me about six months to stop worrying and to trust that I was where I was supposed to be. If I'm running late and stuck in traffic, instead of stressing out, I now believe there's a reason for the delay. Maybe it's avoiding an accident or to give me a moment of quiet reflection. Whatever the reason, I've learned to trust the process and focus on the next step rather than trying to control every aspect of the outcome.

Delusional thinking is about more than setting big goals—it's cultivating a mindset that embraces possibility and refuses to be constrained by conventional wisdom or current limitations. By thinking beyond limits, challenging the status quo, and setting audacious goals, you can unlock your full potential and achieve what others might consider impossible.

But what is required to apply delusional thinking in real life? It starts with a willingness to dream a big vision and a commitment to act on the belief that achieving your goal is inevitable. It's about being open to new ideas, embracing uncertainty, and staying focused on your vision, even when the path ahead is unclear.

One of the most effective ways to apply delusional thinking is to surround yourself with people who support and inspire you. Find mentors, colleagues, or friends who share your passion for big ideas and who can offer guidance and encouragement along the way. By building a strong support system, you create an environment that nurtures your delusional thinking and helps you stay motivated and focused.

Another important aspect of applying delusional thinking is to be patient and persistent. Achieving big goals takes time, and setbacks and challenges will inevitably come along the way. But by staying committed to your vision and continuing to take bold steps forward, you can overcome these obstacles and achieve your DUMB goals.

Practical Exercises to Cultivate Delusional Thinking

Now that you understand the importance of delusional thinking, it's time to put it into practice. Here are some exercises that can help you cultivate this mindset:

- **Mind Mapping**: Start by writing a big goal or dream in the center of a page. Then, draw branches out from the center and write all the ideas, possibilities, and steps you can think of to achieve that goal. Don't limit yourself—let your imagination run wild. This exercise helps you explore different angles and possibilities you might not have considered otherwise.

- **Vision Boarding**: Create a visual representation of your big goals and dreams. Gather images, quotes, and symbols that inspire you and arrange them on a board. Place this vision board somewhere you'll see it every day. It will constantly remind you of your goals and keep you focused on what you want to achieve.

- **Role-Playing**: Imagine yourself as the person who has already achieved your delusional goal. How do you act? How do you make decisions? What challenges have you overcome? By stepping into this role, you can gain insights into the mindset and actions needed to turn your dreams into reality.

- **Challenge Assumptions**: Take a current project or goal and identify your assumptions about what's possible. Then, challenge each one. Ask yourself, "What if this assumption isn't true? What if there's another way?" This exercise helps you break free from conventional thinking and opens up new possibilities.

- **Dream Journaling**: Spend a few minutes each day writing down your most significant, audacious dreams. Don't worry about how realistic they are—just let your imagination flow. Over time, you'll start to see patterns and connections that can guide you in setting and achieving your DUMB goals.

The Role of Failure in Delusional Thinking

Delusional thinking isn't about ignoring the possibility of failure but reframing failure as a steppingstone to success. When you set audacious goals, failure is almost inevitable at some point in the journey. However, how you respond to that failure determines your ultimate success.

Thomas Edison famously failed thousands of times before successfully inventing the electric light bulb. When asked about his failures, he reportedly said, "I have not failed. I've just found 10,000 ways that won't work." This mindset is a perfect example of delusional thinking in action. Instead of seeing failure as a dead-end, Edison viewed it as valuable information that brought him closer to his goal.

When you embrace delusional thinking, you must also embrace the idea that failure is a natural part of the process. Each setback is an opportunity to learn, to adjust your approach, and to come back stronger. Maintaining a positive and resilient mindset can turn failures into opportunities for growth and innovation.

The Influence of Environment on Delusional Thinking

Your environment is crucial in shaping your mindset and ability to think delusionally. If you surround yourself with people who are negative, risk-averse, or stuck in conventional thinking, it will be much harder to cultivate a mindset of possibility and innovation.

If you surround yourself with optimistic, creative, and supportive people, you'll find it easier to think big and take bold actions. Seek environments that encourage experimentation, celebrate creativity, and support growth. This environment could be a physical space, like a creative workspace, or a community of like-minded individuals who share your passion for innovation.

In my own life, I've made it a priority to build a network of mentors, colleagues, and friends who inspire and challenge me. These people believe in big ideas and aren't afraid to take risks. Their energy and enthusiasm are contagious, and they help me stay focused on my vision, even when the journey gets tough.

How to Start Thinking Delusionally Today

You don't need to wait for the perfect moment to think delusionally. Here are some simple steps you can take today to begin cultivating this mindset:

- **DUMB Goals**: Think of something you've always wanted to achieve but have been too afraid to pursue. Write it down and commit to taking the first step toward making it a reality.

- **Surround Yourself with Positivity**: Identify the people who support and encourage your dreams. Spend more time with them and limit your exposure to those who bring you down or discourage your ambitions.

- **Embrace Uncertainty**: Instead of fearing the unknown, embrace it as an opportunity for growth and discovery. Trust that the journey will unfold as it's meant to and focus on taking one step at a time.

- **Celebrate Small Wins**: As you work toward your delusional goals, celebrate the small victories along the way. Each step forward is progress; acknowledging these wins will motivate and inspire you.

- **Stay Curious**: Ask questions, explore new ideas, and challenge the status quo. Curiosity is the fuel for innovation, and it will help you stay open to new possibilities and opportunities.

Embracing Delusional Thinking in the Workplace

Delusional thinking isn't just for personal goals; it can also be a powerful tool in the workplace. Organizations that embrace bold, visionary thinking at the forefront of their industries. When companies encourage their teams to think beyond the conventional and challenge the status quo, they open the door to innovation, creativity, and groundbreaking solutions.

Take, for example, a well-known tech company that embraced delusional thinking by setting a seemingly impossible goal: to create a device that could be a phone, camera, music player, and internet browser all in one. This idea seemed absurd at the time—no one had ever combined so many functions into a single device. But by fostering a culture of DUMB goals—Delusional, Uncomfortable, pushing to Move Out of comfort zones, and overcoming Blocks—the company turned this wild vision into reality. The result? The creation of the smartphone, a product that revolutionized not just the tech industry but the way we live our daily lives.

Incorporating delusional thinking into your work environment means fostering a culture where you welcome big ideas and risks are seen as opportunities for growth. It's about encouraging your team to set DUMB goals that stretch their capabilities and challenge them to think outside the box. This mindset doesn't just drive individual success; it can propel an entire organization toward new heights.

Whether leading a team, managing a project, or driving your entrepreneurial venture, delusional thinking can be the key to unlocking your full potential and achieving extraordinary outcomes. By applying the principles of DUMB goals in the workplace, you create an environment where innovation thrives, employees are motivated to push beyond their limits, and the impossible becomes possible.

Remember that delusional thinking is not about losing touch with reality, but about daring to imagine a reality far beyond what's currently conceivable. It's about setting goals that scare you a little—or a lot—and then taking the bold steps necessary to achieve them. Whether in your personal life or at work, embracing this mindset can transform how you approach challenges and opportunities.

As you move forward, don't be afraid to think big—no, think DUMB. Let your imagination run wild, set goals that push you out of your comfort zone, and create the future you truly want to live in. The journey may be daunting, but the rewards of delusional thinking are well worth the effort. Now is the time to take action, move out, and break through the blocks holding you back. Your extraordinary future starts with the bold steps you take today.

CHAPTER 3

The Uncomfortable Zone

The Uncomfortable Zone

Getting comfortable with being uncomfortable is a phrase that's easy to say but far more challenging to live. Yet, this concept is essential when pursuing DUMB goals, the kind that stretches your imagination and pushes you to the limits of your abilities. Whether you're introverted or extroverted, thrive on social interaction, or prefer the quiet of your own company, we all face discomfort in life. In those moments of uncertainty, fear, and even doubt, we find the greatest opportunities for growth.

For me, life—whether as a wife, mother, military officer, corporate leader, or entrepreneur—I've had many moments when I had no idea what I was doing. Each of these roles brought with it a unique set of challenges that were both exciting and terrifying. But as overwhelming as these experiences were, I wouldn't change them for the world. They forced me out of my comfort zone, made me face my fears, and taught me that actual growth happens when we embrace the unknown.

For example, becoming a parent is one of the most exciting and terrifying experiences of my life. I had no idea what I was doing but knew it would be worth it. I did not read any books on parenting as

I knew I had the internet to reference. I chose only to take advice from individuals I trusted, and at the end of the day, I figured it out. My children continue to get me out of my comfort zone and I strive to be a better mom every day.

The Power of Discomfort

Most people view discomfort negatively—something to be avoided or minimized. But what if we shifted our perspective and saw discomfort as a sign that we're on the right path? When you're comfortable, you're likely in a space of familiarity, doing things you've done before with little risk or challenge. But when you're uncomfortable, it's because you're stepping into new territory—trying something different, pushing your limits, or tackling a challenge you're not entirely sure you can handle.

Think back to any significant achievement in your life. Chances are, it involved some level of discomfort. Maybe it was the nerves before a big presentation, the fear of failure when starting a new job, or the anxiety of moving to a new city. These feelings of discomfort are natural and often accompanied by growth. Pushing through the discomfort makes you stronger, more capable, and better prepared for the next challenge.

For me, discomfort was a constant companion when I joined the military. As a nuclear missile officer, I was thrust into a world of high stakes and high pressure, where every decision had significant consequences. There were moments when I felt completely out of my depth, wondering if I was cut out for the role. But it was in those moments of uncertainty that I grew the most. I learned to trust my instincts, stay calm under pressure, and lead confidently, even when I didn't have all the answers.

I remember my first Deputy Missile Combat Crew member, whom I helped train and then pull alerts with, once remarked on how calm I seemed after a particularly high-stress situation. It started when we arrived at our Launch Control Center at the beginning of an alert (24-hour shift). We found that at crew changeover, we were taking over one of our Colonels—the Group Commander, essentially my boss's boss. That changeover felt like it lasted forever, but we handled it smoothly. We wanted to leave a good impression that we were a strong, competent crew and that our Group Commander could rely on us for small and large challenges.

The next day, an evaluation crew who came for their Alert also had the responsibility to evaluate us during our daily changeover before signing for the missiles. Their job was to assess how we managed our Launch Control Center and our responsibilities in the missile field. Our technology was old but reliable, but on that day, only one of our two phones was working.

My deputy was still new, so we switched seats so she could handle the phone calls for maintenance actions at three missile sites. I guided her through the process and simultaneously accomplished the evaluation crew's changeover. While things seemed smooth on the surface, I could see the look of fear in my deputy's eyes of doing something wrong while processing her phone calls with the maintenance team and asking the wrong questions while being assessed by the evaluation crew.

Afterward, we returned topside from our underground Launch Control Center up the long elevator about 100 feet to sunlight—and loaded our gear into the crew vehicle.

As we drove down the gravel road, my deputy turned to me and said, "You looked so calm, how did you do that?" I smiled and said, "My uniform t-shirt under my flight suit is completely soaked in sweat." We laughed, then I shared with her the most important lesson. "Breathe, ask questions, work together, and remember that you're not alone. It is important to control your face and body, even if you are sweating underneath."

This key is embracing the discomfort we face when stepping into the uncomfortable zone. On the inside, you may be sweating in fear, but on the outside, show a calm exterior until calm is felt on the inside. Look at fear dead in the eye and say, "Fuck fear, let's go!"

Introversion and the Uncomfortable Zone

As an introverted extrovert—a person who enjoys interacting with people but needs to recharge their energy after social interactions—the idea of getting comfortable with discomfort can be particularly daunting. Introverts often find solace in solitude, reflection, and working behind the scenes rather than being in the spotlight. This is one reason I love being behind the camera, not in front of it. However, stepping into the uncomfortable zone doesn't mean you have to change who you are; it means recognizing that discomfort is part of the process of growth, even for introverts.

Extroverts, too, get nervous and anxious occasionally, but they can often hide it better and approach strangers easily. My extroverted side has no problem asking questions when it is for someone else, like my children or teammates. However, I found that I must be extremely extroverted in my business for it to succeed. As the artist, this means being the face of the brand in front of the camera for social media. This is well outside my comfort zone, but it is necessary as relationships build companies and brands, not only the product.

When I transitioned from the military to the corporate world, I found myself in environments far outside my comfort zone. In my opinion, corporate leadership styles and foundations mirror those in the military—both emphasize structure, discipline, and clear chains of command. However, coming from a military background and not following what I would call the traditional corporate track directly from college, I felt the need to prove myself every day.

One unexpected challenge was the simple act of changing out of my uniform and into business casual attire. In the military, my uniform was more than just clothing; it symbolized identity and camaraderie. It provided a sense of confidence and acted as an armor that protected and empowered me. Suddenly, without it, I felt like I had lost my swagger and felt fully outside my comfort zone—a sentiment that, as I've discovered through conversations with fellow veterans, is a common experience for many transitioning service members who leave active duty.

This may seem insignificant to someone who hasn't served, but it was a profound shift for me. I no longer felt like myself and struggled to find where I fit within this new corporate landscape. The only times I felt a sense of belonging were when I engaged with the company's robust and supportive veterans' group. They understood the nuances of this transition and provided a community where I could reconnect with parts of my identity that felt lost.

The anxiety over what to wear each day became a daily struggle. A few months into my new role, I began laying out my outfits for the entire week to alleviate some of this stress. Making decisions about clothing, something I had rarely had to think about due to decades in uniform, was unexpectedly overwhelming. In the manufacturing environment where I worked, those on the shop floor and direct supervisors wore uniforms, maintaining a semblance of the structured attire I was accustomed to. However, the office personnel dressed in what I referred to as "normal people" clothes, further highlighting the disparity I felt.

Adopting the mentality of "pretend you're comfortable until you are comfortable" became my coping mechanism. It took me nearly two years after leaving active duty and corporate to walk confidently in business attire. Considering that I had spent nearly 30 years wearing a uniform—from a private Catholic school through my military career—those two years were a reasonable adjustment period.

One of the most valuable lessons I learned throughout this transition was that discomfort doesn't have to be a barrier; instead, it can be a bridge to personal growth and self-discovery. I now have found my signature style, which I love–1940s-50s Chanel and Dior meets John Wick.

As an introverted extrovert, I found ways to navigate these challenges so that they aligned with my natural strengths of being a people person who listens and reads body language very well. I did not force myself to be the loudest voice in the room as I learned from the military, and focused on active listening and making thoughtful contributions when I spoke. This approach respected my introverted nature and allowed me to build credibility and trust with my colleagues.

Preparation became another critical strategy. I dedicated ample time to thoroughly prepare for meetings and presentations, which helped me feel more confident and in control, reducing any anxiety from learning new systems. I also ensured I carved out time for solitude and reflection amidst the bustling corporate environment. However, this took me time to accomplish, as we had a lot of online meetings. I learned to schedule this time on my calendar to prepare for what was next.

As I mentioned, I sought mentorship and support systems within the organization, actively building relationships at all levels, including, but not limited to, the women in leadership and the veterans' group. They offered guidance, shared their experiences of navigating corporate culture, and helped me realize that my unique background was not a hindrance but a strength that offered valuable perspectives and skills that the organization needed.

This journey taught me that continuing to step further out of my comfort zone while challenging was instrumental in my personal and professional growth. It allowed me to build upon my resilience, adaptability, and a deeper understanding of myself. I learned that embracing discomfort doesn't mean abandoning who you are; it means expanding your capacity and discovering new facets of your identity and abilities.

Ultimately, navigating through these uncomfortable experiences equipped me with the confidence and competence to excel in diverse environments, whether in the corporate world or as an entrepreneur. It reinforced the idea that discomfort is not something to be feared but embraced as a catalyst for transformation and success.

The Role of Fear in the Uncomfortable Zone

Fear is often at the heart of discomfort. Fear of failure, fear of judgment, fear of the unknown are all common reactions when we step out of our comfort zones. But fear, like discomfort, can be a powerful motivator if we learn to embrace it rather than shy away.

When I first became an entrepreneur, fear was all around. I was leaving behind the security of a steady paycheck and venturing into uncharted territory. The stakes were high—not just for me, but for my family. There were sleepless nights filled with creation, doubt, and moments when I questioned whether I had made the right decision. But it was in facing these fears that I found the courage to move forward.

One of the most important steps in overcoming fear is to reframe it. Instead of seeing fear as a signal to stop, see it as a sign that you're on the brink of something significant. Fear often arises when we're about to do something that matters—something that can potentially change our lives. By recognizing this, you can use fear as a guide, pushing you toward the actions that will lead to the most growth.

When I was launching GATE 28 & J. Rose Scrolls By Julie Jamison Galleries, there were countless moments when fear threatened to hold me back. The fear of failing in front of my peers, the fear of financial instability, the fear of not living up to my expectations—these were real and present. But instead of letting these fears paralyze me, I acknowledged them, accepted them as part of the process, and kept moving forward even when it felt like the world around me was falling apart. I want you to look at fear dead in the eye and saying, "fuck it, what is the best that could happen!"

Case Study—John F. Kennedy and the Space Race

President John F. Kennedy's bold decision to commit the United States to landing a man on the moon is a powerful example of stepping outside the comfort zone on a grand scale. 1961 when Kennedy announced this ambitious goal, the United States was trailing behind the Soviet Union in the space race. The Soviets had already sent the first human, Yuri Gagarin, into space, and America's space program was still in its infancy.

Many saw this commitment as almost delusional. The technology required to achieve a moon landing didn't exist; the costs were astronomical, and the risks were immense. Yet Kennedy's bold vision pushed the nation out of its comfort zone. He famously stated, "We choose to go to the moon in this decade and do the other things, not because they are easy, but because they are hard."[3]

Kennedy's decision required unprecedented innovation, collaboration, and resourcefulness. NASA had to develop new technologies, solve countless technical challenges, and overcome significant obstacles. The entire endeavor was fraught with uncertainty and discomfort at every level—from the engineers who designed the spacecraft to the astronauts who risked their lives.

However, this commitment to stepping outside the comfort zone paid off. On July 20, 1969, Neil Armstrong became the first human to set foot on the moon, fulfilling Kennedy's vision. The success of the Apollo 11 mission was not just a victory for the United States but a testament to achievement when we dare to push beyond our perceived limits.

This case study illustrates that embracing discomfort on a massive scale can lead to extraordinary achievements. Kennedy's decision to pursue the moon landing challenged the nation to think bigger, work harder, and accomplish something that had previously seemed impossible. It is a powerful reminder that stepping outside our comfort zones, even in the face of overwhelming challenges, can lead to groundbreaking success.

Building Resilience Through Discomfort

Resilience is the ability to bounce back from challenges and setbacks, and it's a trait built through repeated exposure to being uncomfortable. Each time you face a difficult situation and come out on the other side, you're strengthening your resilience. The challenges may not get easier, but you become better equipped to handle them.

In my journey, resilience has been a key factor in my ability to navigate the uncomfortable zones of life.

As a mother, sometimes I felt overwhelmed by the responsibility of raising children while balancing a demanding career. As a military officer, there were days when the pressure seemed unbearable. And as an entrepreneur, there were moments when I doubted whether I had what it took to succeed. But in each of these roles, resilience kept me going. When you have no choice but success, pressing forward is the only option.

One way I've built resilience is by embracing the idea that failure is not the end—it's a learning opportunity. Every setback, mistake, and challenge has something to teach us if we're willing to look for the lesson. This mindset has allowed me to approach discomfort with curiosity rather than fear, asking myself, *What can I learn from this experience? How can this make me stronger?*

For instance, early in my entrepreneurial journey, I focused on releasing only 28 art photographs on the 28th of each month. I decided to set a DUMB Goal for myself and redo my entire website to support this style. I hired a web team that supports artists and builds websites in about 30 days. Long story short, my website was off-brand with the luxury market. I had paid thousands of dollars to build a beautiful site, but it did not look up to the five-figure-priced art.

My executive assistant was tactful and said, "Is it okay for me to be honest? Your site does not match your high-ticket artwork." I told her I completely agreed and pulled an all-nighter to build what I envisioned myself. I expanded by limiting my target market to art collectors, luxury interior designers, and four- and five-star hotel owners. My online galleries are the first thing they see. Branding must align. I learned a ton about building a website. I believe it is important to learn the behind-the-scenes process of your business as you build. However, I also learned that you could pay someone a boatload of money, but that does not mean they will deliver on their promise. This made me always want the best for my clients because we all deserve to be treated well regardless of the price tag.

Embracing the Uncomfortable Zone

Growth and success often lie beyond the boundaries of comfort. Embracing discomfort is not just about enduring challenges—it's about actively seeking them out as opportunities for growth. Here are five powerful strategies to help you thrive in an uncomfortable zone.

1. Set Stretch Delusional Goals

Stretch Delusional goals push you to aim higher than you thought possible. These intentionally ambitious goals are just beyond your current capabilities, compelling you to grow and adapt. By setting stretch delusional goals, you're challenging yourself and expanding your belief in what you can achieve. The discomfort of pursuing these goals is a sign that you're on the right path.

2. Develop Resilience Through Discomfort

Resilience is built through repeated exposure to discomfort. By consistently stepping into situations that challenge you, whether public speaking, taking on difficult projects, or learning new skills, you gradually build the mental and emotional toughness needed to handle more significant challenges. Each time you face discomfort, you're strengthening your ability to cope with it in the future.

3. Reframe Discomfort as a Learning Opportunity

Instead of seeing discomfort as something to be avoided, reframe it as a learning opportunity. Every uncomfortable experience teaches you something valuable about yourself, your capabilities, and your world. This mindset shift allows you to approach challenges with curiosity rather than fear, transforming discomfort into a tool for personal growth.

Here are some starting questions to think deeper:

- When was the last time you felt discomfort while pursuing a goal? What did that experience teach you?

- How do you typically respond to discomfort—do you lean into it, or do you avoid it?

- What might you learn about yourself if you viewed discomfort as a sign of growth rather than a signal to stop?

4. Leverage the Power of Incremental Progress

Significant changes often start with small steps. Break down daunting challenges into manageable tasks and focus on making consistent, incremental progress. This approach makes large goals more achievable and helps you build confidence as you see tangible results. Each small victory reinforces your ability to navigate discomfort and continue moving forward.

5. Seek Out New Challenges Regularly

Make a habit of seeking new challenges that push you beyond your comfort zone. Whether taking on a project outside your usual scope, engaging in difficult conversations, or trying something entirely new, regularly confronting discomfort ensures continuous growth. By embracing challenges as a part of your routine, you become more adaptable and better equipped to handle whatever life throws your way.

The Uncomfortable Zone in Action

When I was preparing to transition from the military to the corporate world, I was stepping into a completely unfamiliar environment. The military had been my life for over a decade—it was structured, disciplined, and focused on team success. Although the corporate world seemed different from the outside looking in, it was the same. It just took me time to recognize it.

I was repeatedly told, "Since you're new to manufacturing...." I allowed this to get to my head and hinder my growth. After months of hearing this, I realized I merely manufactured in a different industry. I came from manufacturing future Air Force leaders by instructing; I manufactured team consolidated advice and support for military senior leaders, advising Congress and the President of the United States how to press forward with my operations knowledge. And I manufactured deterrence for the American people every day when in the missile field. I shifted my mindset and allowed myself to realize I had earned my seat at the table; it was time for me to use my voice to a greater capacity. My outside perspective could help me build the company to the next level.

One of the most powerful moments in my journey was when I was offered a leadership role in quality at a company I admired. Having experience in quality management from my military background, I was confident that I had a solid knowledge baseline. However, every organization has its nuances, and this role required me to learn new regulations for the specific manufacturing industry while leaning on my diverse background and resilience to guide me. Trusting my instincts, applying my experience, and adapting to the specific challenges of this new environment was crucial. If it weren't for the patience and support of those within the company who helped me build my knowledge, it might have taken me much longer to make efficient and integrity-based decisions. Their guidance was instrumental in my ability to adapt quickly and effectively, allowing me to integrate my experience with the organization's specific needs and ultimately push myself to new heights.

Redefining Comfort

Comfort is the ability to thrive in the face of discomfort. The more you embrace discomfort, the more you'll find that it becomes less intimidating and more empowering. You'll see discomfort not as something to be avoided but as a necessary part of growth and success.

So, whether you're an introvert or an extrovert, stepping into a new role, launching a business, or pursuing a personal goal, remember that the uncomfortable zone is where the magic happens. It's where you'll find the greatest learning, growth, and transformation opportunities. And as you continue to push through discomfort, you'll discover that you're capable of far more than you ever imagined.

Your journey into the uncomfortable zone won't be easy—it will be filled with challenges, setbacks, and moments of doubt. But it will also be filled with breakthroughs, triumphs, and a deep sense of accomplishment. As Neale Donald Walsch famously said, "Life begins at the end of your comfort zone."[4] So, get comfortable with being uncomfortable, and watch as you achieve goals that once seemed impossible.

CHAPTER 4

Move Out

Move Out

In this chapter, we'll explore the significance of moving forward on your daily goals, even if it's just small steps. We'll discuss overcoming the fear of being unprepared, creating a flexible strategic plan, and building momentum through small wins. We'll cover the importance of resilience, visualization, and surrounding yourself with supportive individuals to ensure you're always progressing toward your ultimate goals.

The Power of Taking Action

The most critical step in pursuing any significant goal is often the simplest: taking action. Whether you're striving to build a successful business, achieving personal growth, or leaving a legacy, the journey always begins with a single step.

The military uses the term "move out" to signify stepping out of the planning stage and taking deliberate action. Moving out is doing the actions needed to reach your goals and turn your dreams and aspirations into tangible realities.

Tony Robbins, the renowned motivational speaker and life coach, emphasizes the importance of immediate action. He often says, "The path to success is to take massive, determined action."[5] Robbins' message is clear: success comes not from waiting for the perfect moment, but from taking steps toward your goals today, even if you feel only partially prepared. It's not about faking it till you make it. That refers to pretending to be confident or skilled in something until you achieve that level of competence. However, the more powerful approach is to "live it until you are it"—fully adopting the mindset, habits, and behaviors of your future self, acting as if you've already reached your goals, which helps you grow into that reality.

The concept of "move out" resonates deeply with anyone who has ever felt the paralysis of over-planning. It's about breaking free from the cycle of hesitation and doubt and embracing the power of now. None of us are guaranteed tomorrow. If not today, when? You don't need to have every detail figured out before you start—you just need to know the first step. What's crucial is that you begin, trusting that clarity and confidence will follow as you make progress.

I am a determined person with Type A tendencies, meaning I always want a plan to press forward with decisions. When I began my entrepreneurial journey, I quickly realized that being Type A wasn't sustainable for me long-term in pursuing my DUMB goals. The concept of Type A personality, introduced by cardiologists Dr. Meyer Friedman and Dr. Ray Rosenman in the 1950s, describes individuals who are highly competitive, ambitious, and organized, often driven by a sense of urgency. While these traits can be strengths, Type A personalities are also prone to stress, impatience, and health risks if not managed properly.[6]

The reason I bring this up, aside from the health concerns, is because, for the first time in my life, I am taking the leap to build GATE 28 & J. Rose Scrolls Galleries didn't come with a clear success plan; I had to make it up as I went. In traditional American schooling, to be successful we attend classes for ten months out of the year, five days a week, with a clear daily schedule of the learning objectives to reach the next level. But when you start your own company, you are the one creating the blueprint for your success. You have to continually evaluate: Am I doing what I truly want? Am I becoming a better person? Do my actions align with where I want to be in three months, a year, or three years from today?

I am grateful for the entrepreneurs I connected with early on. My sister-in-law, Amy Traugh, for example, had started two companies during COVID. When I told her I had officially left the safety net of corporate life and was terrified of how I'd support our family with four young children, she immediately congratulated me. As a three-time female founder, business strategist, #1 Amazon best-selling author of *The CEO Method*, wife, and mother of two, she understood my seemingly delusional DUMB goals. Her best advice was to set clear deliverables for each day, week, and month—and follow through on those.

It took me about seven to eight months to build a daily schedule that supported scaling the company and brand. This included time blocking my calendar and scheduling every task—meetings, photoshoots, driving time, school drop-offs, and even brain-off time for sleep. Yes, I schedule everything, seven days a week. Doing this attracted more business relationships and helped me feel calmer because I created a regimen that worked for me. There are days when I throw the schedule out the window to take longer on a photoshoot because the weather, location, and light are just perfect. I've learned to stop saying I'm busy and start saying I'm living life to the fullest. I've also learned not to take on others' battles that aren't mine to fight—a large but necessary adjustment. Since childhood, I've always felt responsible for helping everyone, even when they didn't ask for it.

Understanding the difference between a company and a brand is crucial in business development. A company refers to a legal entity or organization that provides products or services intending to make a profit. It is structured to manage resources, operations, and strategies for financial success.

On the other hand, a brand represents the emotional connection and perception consumers have with a product or company. It includes the values, image, and reputation that are crafted over time through marketing, design, and customer experience. While a company operates for profit, a brand seeks to build loyalty and trust with its audience.[7]

How do I make more time on my calendar? I ask myself: *Is this my battle? Is it my husband's or children's battle? If so, should I be there to listen, guide, or let them figure it out?* This doesn't mean withdrawing from relationships, but setting boundaries because time is precious, and we all deserve to respect it. Of course, if it's a dangerous or life-threatening situation, I'll do whatever I can to help. But for everyday issues, I've learned to, in the famous words of Elsa, "Let it go."

The Importance of Daily Progress: One Step at a Time

When I first embarked on my entrepreneurial journey, I didn't have all the answers. There were many days when I felt like I had no idea what I was doing, but I accomplished the required tasks anyway. The key was taking that first step and then the next, trusting that each action would bring me closer to my goal. My initial ambitions were simple yet meaningful: I wanted full-time flexibility, the freedom to pick up my children from school, and the joy of wearing stretchy pants because they symbolized independence. These weren't grandiose aspirations, but they were important to me.

Each day, I committed to taking at least one step toward my goals, no matter how small. Some days, it was as simple as making a phone call or emailing. On other days, it involved brainstorming new ideas using the mind mapping method we walked through earlier or learning something new. Progress doesn't have to be monumental; it just needs to be consistent. As the saying goes, "The journey of a thousand miles begins with a single step."

This daily commitment to progress sets successful people apart. We often look at successful individuals and wonder, *How did they do it?* The answer lies in their ability to take consistent, purposeful action. They don't wait for the perfect moment or for all the stars to align; they move forward, trusting each step will lead them closer to their goal. Successful people are no more or less than you, they put their pants on one leg at a time. The real difference is they chose to be successful.

Taking one step a day soon becomes your new comfort zone, so you must force yourself back into the uncomfortable zone. For example, if yesterday you made contact with one museum to showcase your artwork, and it is no longer as scary as you thought, make sure today you contact two to three museums.

We all know that the first phone call or email is the hardest. When I was in technical training after being commissioned into the Air Force, it took me about three months to feel comfortable picking up a phone and asking a quick question. Technical training is our specialized schooling for your career field at the beginning of your career to learn the job basics before heading to your full-time unit, most likely at another base location. Part of my role was to connect our missile maintainers from the missile to our base for updates on their actions using our push button landline phone. I remember writing every phone call during training, essentially a script, before connecting with them so I didn't sound like I did not know what I was doing. This seems simple, but texting had just become unlimited when I was leaving college. Yes, for anyone born after the year 2000, let me educate you. Back in the late 1900s, phone companies limited how many texts you could make per month, so, we still called people. I digress. Once I was comfortable with this, I went back to my uncomfortable zone and learned how to have an open dialogue without a script.

Research also supports the concept of taking daily action, however small. According to a study published in the Journal of Applied Psychology[8] individuals who set daily goals and made small, incremental progress toward those goals were more likely to achieve long-term success. The study found that these daily actions helped individuals stay motivated, maintain focus, and build momentum, ultimately leading to the achievement of larger goals.[9]

Overcoming the Fear of Not Being Ready

One of the biggest obstacles to taking action is the fear of needing more time to be ready. It's easy to convince ourselves that we need more time, experience, or resources before we can start working toward our goals. But if we wait until we feel 100% ready, we may never take that first step.

I wasn't fully prepared when I started GATE 28 & J.Rose Scrolls By Julie Jamison Galleries. I didn't have a detailed business plan, but I knew I would never start if I waited until everything was perfect. Instead, I embraced the uncertainty and took action anyway. I applied for opportunities that seemed out of reach and pursued projects I wasn't entirely sure I could handle. I embodied the mindset and behaviors of who I wanted to become. I lived as if I were already the successful business owner I aspired to be, and in doing so, I created my present and future state, what I call my family empire.

This approach is echoed by Tony Robbins, who advises people to "take action immediately—before fear has time to set in" (Robbins, 2014). By taking action, even when you feel unprepared, you build confidence and momentum. You prove to yourself you're capable of more than you initially thought, and this realization empowers you to keep moving forward.

Becoming a parent is a good example. I was the first in my group of girlfriends to become a mom. The two pieces of advice I gave them about being a mom were: Trust your instincts, and it's your baby and your rules. You know what's best, so don't listen to anyone's advice.

Starting a business is the same—there's no perfect blueprint or guaranteed path to success. Just like parenting, trusting your instincts and following your vision is key to building a business that reflects your values and goals.

Overcoming the fear of not being ready also requires a mindset shift. Instead of focusing on what you lack or what could go wrong, focus on what you have and can do today. This may be as simple as taking a five-minute walk outside because your goal is to focus on moving more during the day. This shift in perspective can help you move past fear and take steps toward your goals. Remember, it's not about being perfect; it's about making progress.

Creating a Strategic Plan: Turning Dreams into Reality

When embarking on any significant journey, a strategic plan is your roadmap that guides you toward your goals. It's the foundation that keeps you focused, motivated, and on track. However, one critical lesson I've learned—and one that many driven individuals must grapple with—is that your strategic plan doesn't always need to be clear-cut to reach your delusional goals. As a Type A personality, a plan-every-detail-in-my-life type of leader, wife, and mom, accepting this ambiguity was a big pill to swallow.

In the military, we pride ourselves on the concept of "train like you fight," which means our training simulates real-life scenarios as closely as possible. This rigorous preparation ensures that we remain calm under pressure, and no one is left panicking when things go awry. Sure, you might want to vomit after the fact, but during the heat of the moment, you thrive under pressure, similar to the process that turns carbon into a diamond.

However, when pursuing personal goals or launching a business, the rigid, detail-oriented approach I had always relied on had to be softened. Instead of having every step mapped out, I had to learn to embrace uncertainty and stay open to evolving ideas. My strategic goals became more about the broader vision than the nitty-gritty details.

When I began my journey as an entrepreneur, I knew I wanted to help people in a way that connected to my art. Was this goal vague? Absolutely. But that's precisely the point. By keeping my goal broad, I allowed myself the flexibility to explore various paths and discover new opportunities along the way.

I also applied this principle to publishing a book. I knew I wanted to write a book, but I didn't have a fully fleshed-out plan from the start. What I knew was that I would call it *DUMB Goals*. Over time, I started and stopped multiple versions of the book, outlining how I thought it would flow. I walked away from my concept for months before returning with a fresh perspective. It was not till I felt fully comfortable with stepping way outside my comfort zone that I decided, That's it. Today is the day to finalize this book. It was time to hire an editor and publisher and set a release date. I didn't rush to complete it in one go; instead, I took it step by step. I reached out to my network and asked if anyone knew an editor. When I found one, I didn't immediately dive into intense work or even hire them. I sat on the idea for about 4-6 weeks, letting it marinate. Yet, during this period, I kept announcing to everyone I was writing a book. The act of verbalizing my goal kept it alive and present in my mind, even if I wasn't actively diving deep into all the nuances.

Eventually, the moment came when I had to act. I blocked my calendar in between children's activities, photo shoots, hiring a sales team, executive assistant, website/brand designer, and social media support. I gave myself 72 hours and did everything I could to "brain dump" the concept on paper, even though this final book is much different from the first draft.

Brain dumping is a useful technique to quickly and freely transfer all the thoughts, ideas, worries, tasks, and other mental clutter from your mind onto paper. The goal is to clear your mind by capturing everything occupying your mental space, making it easier to focus, organize, and prioritize. I knew the first draft would not be the final draft, but I needed to get my ideas out, even if they were not my best work.

When I told my editor that my goal was to release the book on my one year business anniversary, she acknowledged that it would be tight but not impossible. Surrounding myself with people who say, "It may not be easy, but let's do it," was vital to making this happen. Thank you, Keren, for believing in me to meet my delusional DUMB Goal of releasing about six weeks after we partnered.

This experience taught me I knew my end state vision months before seeing how I would accomplish the goal. To be honest, I am happy I did not write this book immediately after leaving corporate. I believe my growth in personal development and leadership was essential before finishing the book's message. Your goals can evolve as you do, and sometimes, the most powerful goals are the ones that remain open to interpretation. The clarity comes not from having every detail mapped out from the beginning but from allowing yourself the space to adapt and grow.

Building Momentum Through Small Wins

Building momentum is crucial in any endeavor, and small wins play a significant role in maintaining that momentum. When working toward a goal, especially one that feels monumental, it's easy to get overwhelmed by the enormity of the task ahead. However, by breaking your goal into smaller, more manageable tasks, you create opportunities for success.

These small wins are essential for a few reasons. First, they provide a sense of accomplishment, which boosts your confidence and motivation. Every time you check a task off your list, no matter how small, you reinforce the belief that you can achieve your larger goal. This positive reinforcement creates a feedback loop, where each success fuels further action.

When I accomplish a task as simple as loading the dishwasher and cleaning the kitchen, If I have my planner out, I will even write my "to-done" list just to cross it off. I had to take the time to learn this and stop saying, "I got nothing done today, I have so much to do, or I am behind." This is one area where, to this day, I continue to shift my vocabulary to tell myself, *I am so productive, I am able to accomplish my tasks easily and efficiently.* Yes, these sound like affirmations, and they work to support reprogramming your thinking.

Second, small wins build momentum. Just as a snowball rolling downhill gains speed and size, your progress accelerates as you accumulate more small victories. Over time, these small wins compound, leading to significant progress and, eventually, achieving your goal.

For instance, when I decided to integrate nature into my daily routine, I didn't start with a goal of hiking five days a week. I began by stepping outside and going for a walk, regardless of the weather. Each walk, each step, was a small win that built my confidence and made the next walk or hike easier. As I continued, these small victories added up, and before long, hiking became a regular part of my life, rain or shine.

Small wins also help you stay focused and motivated during the more challenging phases of your journey. When you encounter obstacles or setbacks, reflecting on your previous successes can remind you how far you've come and give you the strength to keep going.

A study published in *The European Journal of Social Psychology* found that people who celebrated small wins were more likely to maintain long-term motivation and achieve their goals. The study highlighted that acknowledging even minor achievements can create a sense of progress and fulfillment, which is critical for sustaining effort over time.[10]

Adjusting Your Course Without Losing Sight of the Goal

While having a strategic plan is essential, it's equally important to remain flexible and willing to adjust your course as needed. The path to success is rarely linear, and you will inevitably encounter detours, setbacks, and unexpected challenges along the way. The key is to stay focused on your ultimate goal while being open to new opportunities and willing to change your approach when necessary.

The ability to adapt and pivot has been crucial to my success. When I started my company, I had a clear vision of what I wanted to achieve, but I also understood that getting there would take a lot of work. There have been many times when I faced challenges because I was offering something few artists or photographers do with their work. Exclusive 1 of 1 Fine Art Photography is a concept rare in photography in the digital world. I knew it was part of my vision and important for each client to have a one-of-a-kind photography piece. Choosing this unknown path challenged me to create my best artwork and be patient while those around me learned about my strong vision and made this my compass in all my decisions.

For example, when I began taking photographs of flowers and experimenting with AI, I had no idea that it would eventually lead to a successful business. My initial goal was to explore my passion for photography as an artist and create something new that I would be proud to hang up in my home. But as I continued to experiment and push myself, new opportunities emerged. I realized I could turn my passion into a business, and I adjusted my course accordingly.

This ability to adapt and pivot is crucial to long-term success. It's important to remain committed to your vision while being open to new possibilities and willing to change your approach when necessary. As the saying goes, "The only constant in life is change," and your ability to navigate change will determine your success.

This is where surrounding yourself with a supportive network becomes vital. When you need to pivot or adjust your course when your instincts tell you this is the right path. Having people who encourage you to stay focused on the end goal—rather than getting bogged down in the details—can make all the difference. These individuals will remind you that while the journey may not be easy, it's worth the effort.

The Power of Visualization: Living as Your Future Self

Visualization is a powerful tool that many successful individuals use to reach their goals. It is a tool that can help you stay focused and motivated as you work toward your vision. By creating a mental image of your desired outcome and imagining yourself living that reality, you align your thoughts, emotions, and actions with your goals, making it easier to take the necessary steps to achieve them.

When I first started my company, GATE 28 & J. Rose Scrolls By Julie Jamison Galleries, I used visualization to help me stay focused and motivated. I imagined myself living the life I wanted—running a successful business, having the flexibility to spend time with my family, and feeling fulfilled by my work. I visualized the details of my ideal day from the moment I woke up to the activities I engaged in. This practice helped me stay connected to my goals and made taking action easier, even when I felt uncertain or overwhelmed.

One simple way I visualized my future state was by stepping back into business dress clothes, even when I was home. I did this overnight and said I wanted to look and feel more put together for me. This all sprung from changing my title on my LinkedIn account a few months prior. I was afraid to give myself the title of Founder, CEO & Fine Art Photographer. Previously, I was the Owner, Creative Lead Photographer. Both worked well, but Founder, CEO & Fine Art Photographer made more sense and told individuals roughly what I do.

I was traveling to South Hampton, NY, after being accepted to exhibit, when I realized I needed to ask myself, *Who is my true target client? Who am I when I walk in the room and introduce myself?* My client is an individual who loves fine art as a collector, supports their clients such as an art dealer or luxury interior designer, and is searching for the perfect cohesive feel for their luxury home, office, or hotel.

Something clicked in my head when I made this change. I remember being afraid to state that I was a photographer on my LinkedIn account, coming from years of technical training and years of leadership in both the military and corporate. Why? Because in my head, people were paying attention to what I was doing. When, most likely, they were in their own world living their life. I remember taking a few days to commit to placing the title "Owner, Creative

Lead Photographer" at the beginning of my vision. Fast forward about eight months, and I updated the Linked In in about a minute to "Founder, CEO & Fine Art Photographer." I remember telling my husband shortly after, "I love being my own boss, I just promoted myself." We laughed as I ordered new business cards for the Hamptons Fine Art Fair we were attending in a few months.

This led to a chain reaction of action over the next couple of months. One I thought of for some time was, *Am I priced appropriately?* When we were in the Hamptons, my husband and I realized quickly, even after months of continued research on base value in artwork, my work was severely underpriced since I created exclusive 1-of-1 fine art photography prints. I remember discussing with my husband the best time to increase base value, and we decided six months at the earliest. Once I hired my sales team, I asked if it would be difficult to increase our sales quota if I increased the base value six weeks earlier than I planned. They did not object, so I increased the base value that week. Like I mentioned earlier, "If not now, when?"

Research has shown that visualization can be a powerful tool for achieving goals. A study conducted by the University of California, Los Angeles (UCLA)[11] found that participants who practiced visualization performed better in tasks and achieved their goals more effectively than those who did not. Visualization helps to prime the brain for success by activating the neural pathways associated with the desired behavior or outcome.

By visualizing yourself as your future self today, you embody the mindset, habits, and actions that will lead you to your goals. You live as if you've already achieved your desired outcome, making it more likely that you will achieve it.

This practice of *living as if* is not about pretending or faking it; it's about aligning your current actions with the life you want to create. When you act in accordance with your future self's mindset, you make decisions and take actions that move you closer to your goals. Over time, this alignment creates a powerful momentum that propels you forward.

The Role of Resilience in Moving Forward

Resilience is the ability to bounce back from setbacks and continue moving forward despite adversity. When you're working toward ambitious goals, resilience is essential. Sometimes things don't go as planned, when you face unexpected challenges, or when progress seems slow. In these moments, resilience keeps you going.

Building resilience involves developing a mindset that views challenges as opportunities for growth. Instead of seeing setbacks as failures, resilient individuals see them as valuable learning experiences. They understand every obstacle is an opportunity to learn, adapt, and become stronger.

When I was working on expanding my fine art business, there were many occasions when things didn't go as planned. Whether it was a project that didn't turn out as expected to a personal setback, I encountered my fair share of challenges. But each time I reminded myself, I learned a lesson I needed to learn. These challenges and obstacles were part of the process and helped me grow stronger and more capable.

One way to build resilience is to practice self-compassion. When you encounter setbacks, it's important to be kind to yourself and avoid self-criticism and guilt. Recognize that everyone faces challenges on the path to success and that it's okay to make mistakes. Treating yourself with compassion builds the emotional strength needed to persevere.

Think about the last challenge you faced. Write the basic scenario, then ask yourself these questions. *In what ways were you critical toward yourself? How could you have given yourself more compassion?* Then take a moment and rewrite how you could have responded in that scenario. Rewriting history is a great tool for knowing how you will handle situations in the future. It empowers you to move forward.

Another key to resilience is maintaining a sense of purpose. When you connect to your "why"—the deeper reason behind your goals—it becomes easier to stay motivated, even when the going gets tough. Your purpose acts as a compass, helping you navigate challenges and stay focused on your ultimate goal.

Resilience is not just about bouncing back; it's about growing through adversity. Each setback provides an opportunity to learn, adapt, and become stronger. By embracing challenges and viewing them as steppingstones to success, you build the resilience needed to achieve your goals. We will build upon this in Chapter 7.

Building a Support System: Surrounding Yourself with Positivity

No one achieves success alone. Building a support system of mentors, friends, and colleagues who believe in you and your goals is crucial to staying motivated and moving forward. Surrounding yourself with positive, like-minded individuals can provide the encouragement, guidance, and accountability you need to stay on track.

Application: Make a list of people you consider your support team. Write the ways they support you. What other support do you need? Who do you know who could provide that support and reach out to them?

I have been fortunate to have the support of my husband, who believed in my vision and encouraged me to pursue my goals. His support gave me the additional confidence to keep going, even when I faced challenges together. Additionally, I sought out mentors who had experience in the areas I was exploring. Their guidance helped me navigate the complexities of building a business and provided valuable insights I might not have discovered.

Surrounding yourself with positivity also means limiting your exposure to negativity. While it's important to consider constructive feedback, protecting yourself from naysayers who might undermine your confidence or discourage you from pursuing your dreams is equally important. Choosing the people you spend time with creates an environment supporting your growth and success.

Building a support system is also about being there for others. You create a mutual support network by offering encouragement, sharing your experiences, and supporting others in their journeys. This network not only strengthens your relationships but also reinforces your own commitment to your goals.

Taking Responsibility for Your Success

At the end of the day, you are responsible for your success. Taking ownership of your goals and holding yourself accountable for your actions are critical components of moving forward. This requires being honest with yourself about your progress, recognizing when you need to adjust, and taking proactive steps to stay on track.

One way to build accountability is to set clear, measurable goals and regularly review your progress. You can do this through journaling, setting up regular check-ins with a mentor or accountability partner, or using tools like project management software to track your tasks and milestones.

Taking responsibility for your success also means recognizing that your actions, decisions, and mindset directly impact your outcomes. By taking ownership of your journey, you empower yourself to make the necessary changes to achieve your goals.

This level of accountability requires self-discipline and a commitment to personal growth. It's about holding yourself to a high standard and continuously striving to improve. When you take responsibility for your success, you shift from a victim mentality to a empowerment mindset, where you control your destiny.

Returning to the topic of time blocking my calendar. It only works when I consistently use the techniques I learned. For example, it is important for me to be in the moment when I am photographing landscapes and architecture. The first reason is that I want to be in my creative space so my clients can see the beauty I create for them in my work. The second is safety from cliffs or animals. However, being in the moment early on in immersing myself back into nature would turn into hours of me not paying attention to the time. Now, I do my best to stick to the schedule while still allowing myself time to roam free to create my masterpieces.

The Importance of Gratitude and Reflection

As you move forward on your goals, take time to reflect on your progress and practice gratitude. Gratitude is a powerful tool for maintaining a positive mindset and staying motivated. By focusing on what you've achieved and the progress you've made, you reinforce the belief that you can achieve your goals.

Regular reflection allows you to assess your progress, celebrate your wins, and identify areas for improvement. It also provides an opportunity to reconnect with your why and ensure that your actions align with your vision and values.

I'm reminded of the simple goals I set for myself when I started my company—goals like taking and picking up my children from school and bringing peace to myself and my family. These goals may have seemed small, but they laid the foundation for everything that followed. By taking consistent action, embracing uncertainty, and staying connected to my purpose, I built a life that aligns with my values and brings me joy. For example, my sales team asked me what I valued most in my company. I explained that my time was gold; spending time with my family was what I valued most. I told them that 11 am - 2:30 pm during the school year are my set hours of availability Monday through Friday. This includes all meet-and-greet type meetings, meetings with clients, or attending larger networking meetings. As a person who came from never-ending hours of meetings, I do need hours to create the art. Most of the time, this is after dropping off my four children, or after they are tucked in their beds. These are the hours I create specifically to create my fine art photography.

About a week later, I was asked if this time range included Saturdays. I stated that between having four children at home, scheduling their activities, and having designated family time, with advanced notice and a legitimate reason we would need a call, I could be available. I loved my corporate leadership position, but I rarely saw my husband or children. From day one, I did not set a clear boundary that my time was just as valuable as everyone else's. When there is a legitimate emergency, I will drop everything. But it only ended up hurting me being available all the time. Leading impacted my physical and mental health. We do not have to be everything for everyone. I was grateful to have this conversation early in the partnership, as I could verbalize and set the baseline standard of my expectations of respecting my time. As I will ensure the same for them.

Gratitude also plays a crucial role in maintaining motivation and resilience. When you practice gratitude, you shift your focus from what's lacking to what's abundant in your life. This shift in perspective helps you stay positive, even in the face of challenges, and keeps you motivated to keep moving forward.

Conclusion: The Power of Move Out

Move Out is about taking action—every day, one step at a time. It's about overcoming the fear of not being ready, embracing uncertainty, and trusting that each step will bring you closer to your goals. Whether it's building momentum through small wins, visualizing your future self, or adjusting your course as needed, the key is to keep moving forward.

As you progress on your journey, remember that success doesn't come from waiting for the perfect moment or having everything figured out. It's about taking consistent, purposeful action, even when the path is unclear. Embrace the challenges, stay resilient, and rely on your support system to help you navigate the inevitable obstacles.

The power to achieve your dreams lies within your ability to keep moving forward, to take responsibility for your success, and to cultivate gratitude for each step of the journey. So, what can you do today to move out? No action is too small—as long as you take that step. The journey to success begins with a single step, and with each action you take, you are moving closer to the life you've always dreamed of.

CHAPTER 5

Removing Neuroblocks

Removing Neuroblocks

This chapter is your guiding light. It delves into the internal forces that shape your reality. We are all products of our upbringing, our environment, and the societal norms we are taught from birth. Whether you grew up in the United States, Europe, Asia, or anywhere else, your programming—what you've been taught to believe about yourself, your abilities, and your potential—has been influenced by your culture, family, and experiences.

Growing up in a world that emphasized "girl power," I was taught to value independence and to believe that I didn't need a man for anything. This mindset fostered resilience, a strong work ethic, and a sense of self-sufficiency, but it also created a barrier I didn't fully recognize until I started my business. The belief that relying on others, especially my husband, was a sign of weakness became a neuroblock that held me back. It took a significant mental shift to embrace the idea that relying on my partner could be a source of strength rather than a weakness. When I finally let go of this limiting belief and allowed myself to lean on my husband, I discovered a new level of creativity and freedom, realizing that true strength often comes from partnership and support.

Removing those mental roadblocks—those neuroblocks—that prevent you from achieving your true potential is essential. Whether it's a limiting belief, a fear of failure, or a deeply ingrained societal norm, these blocks can be overcome. And the best part? It's easier than you think.

Understanding Neuroblocks: What They Are and Where Do They Come From?

A neuroblock is a mental barrier or limiting belief that prevents you from achieving your full potential. These blocks are often subconscious, meaning you may not even be aware of them. They can manifest in various ways—fear of failure, self-doubt, perfectionism, procrastination, or an unwillingness to take risks. At their core, neuroblocks are rooted in the programming we've received throughout our lives. Understanding these common neuroblocks can help you identify and overcome the obstacles that may be holding you back, enabling you to break free from limiting patterns and move toward your goals with greater clarity and confidence. Here are some examples of common neuro blocks:

1. **Impostor Syndrome:** The persistent belief that you're not as competent as others

perceive you to be, leading to fear of being exposed as a "fraud."[12]

2. **Fear of Success:** The anxiety that achieving success will bring about negative consequences, leading to self-sabotage.[13]

3. **Fixed Mindset:** The belief that abilities and intelligence are static, which discourages effort and learning from mistakes.[14]

4. **Overgeneralization:** A negative conclusion based on a single event or experience, which can prevent future risk-taking.[15]

5. **Catastrophizing:** Exaggerating the potential negative outcomes of a situation, leading to paralyzing fear and inaction.[16]

6. **People-Pleasing:** The compulsion to seek approval from others at the expense of one's own needs and goals.[17]

7. **Lack of Boundaries:** The inability to set and enforce personal limits, leading to burnout and resentment.[18]

8. **Scarcity Mindset:** The belief that there are limited resources or opportunities, leading to competition and fear of sharing.[19]

9. **All-or-Nothing Thinking:** Viewing situations in black-and-white terms, leading to

an inability to recognize partial successes or progress.[20]

10. **Learned Helplessness:** The belief that one has no control over outcomes, often due to repeated exposure to uncontrollable events, leading to passivity.[21]

From birth, we absorb our environment's cultural norms, values, and beliefs. If you had grown up in a different country or culture, your programming would be different. In some cultures, conformity and modesty are highly valued, while individualism and self-promotion are encouraged in others. Depending on how you were raised, the roles of men and women, the expectations placed on children, and the definitions of success vary.

Neuroblocks can be traced back to childhood, often starting as early as three. According to research from the American Psychological Association, children begin to internalize societal norms and expectations at a very young age. These early experiences shape their beliefs about themselves and the world around them. If a child consistently hears they're not good enough or that they should be more realistic, these messages become deeply ingrained and can manifest as neuroblocks in adulthood.[22]

But here's the good news: it's never too late to change these beliefs. Neuroplasticity, the brain's ability to reorganize itself by forming new neural connections, allows us to change our thought patterns and beliefs at any age. Even if you've spent decades believing you cannot achieve your dreams, you can rewire your brain to think differently. You can replace those neuroblocks with empowering beliefs that propel you forward.[23]

Identifying and Challenging Limiting Beliefs

The first step in removing neuroblocks is becoming aware of and identifying the limiting beliefs holding you back. These beliefs often operate below the surface, influencing your thoughts, emotions, and actions without conscious awareness. To identify them, you need to pay attention to the thoughts that come up when you consider pursuing a new goal or taking a risk. Do you hear a voice in your head saying, "You're not good enough," "You don't deserve this," or "You'll never succeed"? These are your limiting beliefs.

Remember when I mentioned changing my title on LinkedIn to Founder, CEO & Fine Art Photographer? When I dug deeper into the common neuroblocks above, I felt impostor syndrome and fear of success. For months, I wrestled with self-doubt, imagining what my former colleagues might think. In my mind, they were saying, "Who does Julie think she is? Why does she think she can go from middle-level supervision to CEO? She's so stuck up." But here's the thing: I never heard anyone say these things. It was all in my head, a neuroblock preventing me from fully stepping into my new role and allowing myself to be successful.

I overcame a significant mental barrier called the Scarcity Mindset during this time. Initially, I found myself saying things like, "People don't buy high-ticket fine art every day," almost to justify any slow periods or challenges I faced in selling my work. This seemingly harmless mindset was rooted in a deep-seated belief that opportunities were limited and that only a select few could experience consistent success in the high-end art market. I didn't realize then that I was projecting my fears and limitations onto my potential clients. By assuming buyers were scarce, I was inadvertently shrinking my market and limiting my potential.

Take a minute and write two or three limiting beliefs you have. Identifying these beliefs is crucial because you can challenge them once you're aware of them. Ask yourself, *Is this belief true? Where did it come from? What evidence do I have to support or refute it?* You'll often find these beliefs based on past experiences, societal expectations, or fears that no longer serve you.

Challenging limiting beliefs requires courage and persistence. It's about recognizing that these beliefs are not facts; they're just thoughts you've allowed to become ingrained over time. By questioning these beliefs and replacing them with more empowering ones, you can break down the neuroblocks holding you back. The simple shift of me telling myself, *My clients buy fine art because they love it and love my causes. I am worth being a financially successful artist and photographer. I know my work changes the world every day and attracts fine art collectors, interior designers, and luxury hotel owners.* These are not cocky or allowing my ego to get too big. It shifted decades if not generations of neuroblocks to allow abundance into my business.

The Power of Visualization to Overcome Blocks

Building upon the discussion in Chapter 4 on Neuroblocks, let's explore what it takes to identify and overcome the barriers that stand between you and your goals using the powerful tool of visualization.

Blocks—whether stemming from self-doubt, fear, procrastination, or external challenges—can sometimes feel insurmountable. However, by leveraging the power of your mind, you can transcend these obstacles and propel yourself toward success.

Visualization isn't just about picturing your desired outcomes; it's about actively reprogramming your subconscious mind to align with those outcomes, dismantling the barriers that hold you back.

The science behind visualization is compelling. Cognitive psychology has long established that the brain doesn't always differentiate between vividly imagined scenarios and real-life experiences.[24] This means that by regularly visualizing yourself overcoming specific blocks or challenges, you can create new neural pathways that make success possible and likely. This process is akin to mental rehearsal, where consistent practice in your mind prepares you for real-world execution.

One of the most significant benefits of visualization is its ability to reframe deeply held beliefs that may be holding you back. Often, the most challenging blocks are not external obstacles, but internalized beliefs about what you can or cannot achieve. These beliefs are ingrained over years of experience, societal conditioning, or personal failures. Visualization offers a way to challenge and change these limiting beliefs by creating new mental associations.

For example, if you've always believed that you're not good at public speaking, this belief likely influences your behavior in situations that require you to speak in front of others. You might avoid these situations, or when you face them, your anxiety might lead to a self-fulfilling prophecy of poor performance. Visualization allows you to break this cycle by repeatedly imagining yourself speaking confidently and effectively in front of an audience. Over time, this mental practice can help you build new neural connections that support a more positive self-concept.

When I first started hiking and taking photographs in our local Cuyahoga Valley National Park, I purposely did not take the unknown paths that looked steep and dangerous. I felt someone was going to pop out of a bush and attack me. I realized then that I may have watched too many cop shows growing up. The thought that women should never be in the woods alone popped into my head daily. On top of this, I would say how much I hate heights. Where did this come from? A close family member said how much they hated heights and feared them growing up. When you hear something at a young age, sometimes you pick up others' fears. Recognizing a block means not blaming others and asking ourselves, *Is this my fear? Is this someone else's fear? Why do I feel this way?*

It took telling myself every day for months that I knew these paths connected, knew I had not hiked a particular path, but I was safe, and that this was fun and exciting, no one would attack me. I certainly wouldn't go into the woods in the dark without bear mace and my phone, but what it did was allow me to enjoy being outside with the fresh air, rain or shine. I trusted my instincts, almost back to how we would have before GPS. When time allows me to roam a bit, I just ask myself if it feels right to go right or left today. Often, my body just goes, and I tell myself okay, let's go this way today. Don't get me wrong, I have had a handful of times where I felt something did not seem right about going down a particular path, and I turned around or said aloud, "Nope, today we are not going this way." The times in life when I told myself, *I'm sure I am overthinking this; I should still head down this path*, have not led me to success personally or professionally. Trust your instincts. It is your subconscious telling you to wake up and pay particular attention to the situation.

This daily practice of trusting my instincts connected deeply to removing mental barriers in other areas of life. It reminded me that when I don't second-guess myself, I can move forward without hesitation or doubt. The same principle applied to recognizing when to move forward on an opportunity or when to step back. By consistently tuning into my instincts, I was able to break through the internal resistance that had held me back.

Visualization can help you strengthen your instincts and develop a growth mindset, propelling you further into the uncomfortable zone. Consistent visualization not only enhances your belief in your abilities but also sharpens your intuition, helping you instinctively navigate challenges. Research by psychologist Carol Dweck has shown that individuals with a growth mindset are more likely to embrace challenges, persist in the face of setbacks, and see effort as the path to mastery. By visualizing yourself overcoming obstacles and achieving your goals, you train both your mind and instincts to respond with confidence, reinforcing the belief that you can grow and improve. This powerful combination of instinct and visualization motivates you to take the necessary actions and move forward with conviction.[25]

Practical Techniques for Effective Visualization

While the concept of visualization may seem straightforward, its effectiveness depends on how you practice it. Here are some practical techniques for your DUMB goals journey to help you make the most of your visualization sessions:

1. **Set Clear Intentions:** Before you begin your visualization practice, it's important to set clear intentions for what you want to achieve. This could be overcoming a specific block, such as procrastination, or working

toward a larger goal, like completing a major project. By clarifying your intentions of what you want, you give your mind a clear target to focus on during your visualization. Research supports that goal clarity signifi-cantly enhances achievement.[26]

2. **Engage All Your Senses:** The more vivid and detailed your visualization, the more powerful it will be. Engage all your senses by imagining not just what you see, but also what you hear, smell, taste, and feel. For example, if you're visualizing yourself giving a successful presentation, imagine the feel of the floor beneath your feet, the sound of your voice, the sight of your audience, the smell of the room, and even the taste of the water you might sip beforehand. This multisensory approach makes your visualization more realistic and impactful.[27]

3. **Use Positive Emotions:** Emotions play a crucial role in visualization. When you visualize your success, focus on the positive emotions you would feel in that moment—joy, pride, confidence, and excitement. These emotions help to reinforce the men-tal associations you're creating and make your visualization more effective. By asso-ciating positive emotions with your desired

outcomes, you make those outcomes more appealing and increase your motivation to achieve them.[28]

4. **Practice Regularly:** Consistency is key to effective visualization. Aim to practice your visualization daily, even if it's just for a few minutes. The more you practice, the stronger the neural pathways associated with your desired outcomes will become. Over time, this consistent practice will help to shift your mindset and behavior, making it easier to overcome the blocks that stand in your way. Notice that working toward your goal does not have to take hours on end. Quality over quantity of time invested is vital to success.[29]

5. **Combine Visualization with Move Out Actions:** While visualization is a powerful tool, it's most effective when combined with action. Use your visualization sessions to prepare for real-life challenges and opportunities. After each session, take concrete steps toward your goal, no matter how small. This combination of mental rehearsal and real-world action creates a feedback loop that accelerates your progress and helps you overcome blocks more effectively.[30] For example, if you want to learn about what it takes to become a bodybuilder

because it was your lifelong dream to be in great shape, you could book a gym session with a personal trainer who has competed in bodybuilding competitions. The key is just one step to Move Out.

Building a Vision

While mental visualization is a powerful tool on its own, creating a vision board can amplify its effects by providing a tangible, visual representation of your goals and aspirations. A vision board serves as a constant reminder of what you're working toward and helps keep your goals at the forefront of your mind, making it easier to stay focused and motivated. It acts as a visual checkpoint, allowing you to recognize and address any roadblocks that may arise along your journey.

What Is a Vision Board?

A vision board is a collage of images, words, and symbols representing your goals, dreams, and desires. It's a physical manifestation of your aspirations, designed to inspire and motivate you whenever you see it. But beyond inspiration, it is a powerful tool for identifying and removing the neuroblocks between you and your goals. The idea behind a vision board is that by regularly looking at images representing your goals, you reinforce your commitment to them and engage your subconscious mind in helping you achieve them.

Vision boards can be as simple or as elaborate as you like. Some people prefer a single board dedicated to all their goals, while others create multiple boards focused on different areas of their life, such as career, health, relationships, and personal growth. Regardless of the format, creating a vision board forces you to confront any limiting beliefs that may hold you back, making it an essential tool in overcoming neuroblocks. The key is to make your vision board reflect what truly matters to you and what you want to attract into your life.

How to Create a Vision Board

Creating a vision board is a personal and creative process that can be both fun and fulfilling. There are many personal ways to do this, from downloading a vision board app, or compiling images in a folder on your phone, to writing a list in a journal. Here's a step-by-step blueprint to help you get started:

- **Define Your DUMB Goals:** Before you collect images and materials for your vision board, take some time to reflect on what you want to achieve. This process will also help you identify any internal roadblocks or doubts that need to be addressed. Consider different areas of your life, such as your career, health, relationships, and personal development. What are your short-term and long-term goals? What do you want to manifest in your life? Write your goals to clarify your vision. From personal to professional, write all of it down.

- **Gather Materials:** Determine if you want to make an actual poster board of images, build in a journal, or download an app to compile images on your phone. Once the decision is made, gather the materials that match your medium of choice. During this process, note any resistance or hesitation you feel—these may be signs of underlying neuroblocks that need to be worked through. If it is a poster, gather images, scissors, glue, pushpins, or tape, depending on the type of board you're using. If you want to use a journal, gather a designated journal and pen. If it is the app, download it immediately, and start following the guided steps.

- **Collect Images and Words:** What are the first ten images that represent what you see as your version of success? Maybe you are dreaming about buying your first home. Gather images of the home you would love. As you select these images, be mindful of any limiting beliefs that arise—do you think, *This is too ambitious,* or *I could never achieve this?* If so, these are the exact blocks your vision board will help you overcome. No matter if it is in or out of budget for your current state, go to an open house for a home that spoke to you. Pull these images together down to the furniture you would want to have in your new home.

- **Organize Your Board:** Once you've gathered your materials, start arranging them on your board. There's no right or wrong way to do this—let your creativity guide you. As you arrange your board, note which images bring up feelings of excitement versus those that might cause discomfort or doubt. These emotions are clues to where your neuroblocks may lie. Group similar goals together, create sections for different areas of your life, or simply arrange the images in a way that feels inspiring and motivating.

Personally, I use the journal method and downloaded an app to organize my goals. The journal is a list from 1-x. I start with 1 and start listing all the things I want out of life. From having a job aligned before leaving active duty to my husband's promotion in his dream role to the car in my driveway. I wrote everything down. This process of writing and reflecting has been invaluable in identifying and breaking through my neuroblocks. You would be amazed how many things I have crossed off my list. More recently, I have added the app to maximize visualization potential.

Add Affirmations and Personal Touches: To make your vision board even more powerful, consider adding affirmations or motivational quotes that resonate with your goals. These affirmations should specifically target the limiting beliefs you've identified, helping to reprogram your subconscious mind to support your goals. You can write these out by hand or print them from a computer. Adding personal touches, such as your own artwork, doodles, or photos, can also make your vision board feel more connected to your unique journey.

I have written quotes and concepts I wanted to ensure ended up in this very book. I have notecards and post-its with many ideas because it was the paper closest to me at the time of the idea. Writing all forms of positive reinforcement has been crucial in overcoming the doubts and fears that once held me back. Going back to the example of buying your dream home, you can tell yourself, *I am so grateful for what I have, but I am excited to be moving into my new home! I love knowing the right home for me is here waiting for me.*

Place Your Vision Board Where You'll See It Often: The key to making your vision board effective is to place it somewhere you'll see it regularly. This could be in your bedroom, office, or any space where you spend a lot of time. The more you look at your vision board, the more you will reinforce your goals and challenge any negative thoughts or beliefs that arise. If it is a journal, carry it with you in your bag or backpack, place it on your desk, or set reminders on your phone to check your board on your app. Reviewing every day, even if only for a few minutes, is important to ingrain it as your new reality.

Using Your Vision Board for Daily Visualization

A vision board is most effective when it's integrated into your daily routine. This regular engagement not only keeps your goals top of mind but also allows you to continually address and remove any blocks that may emerge as you progress. Here are some tips on how to use your vision board as part of your visualization practice:

- **Start Your Day with Visualization:** Begin and end each day by spending a few minutes looking at your vision board. During this time, actively visualize yourself overcoming any challenges or roadblocks that stand in your way. This can be accomplished in the shower to getting dressed in the morning. Imagine how it feels to achieve your goals and experience the success, joy, and fulfillment that comes with it. This practice helps set a positive tone for your day and before you sleep to keep your goals top of mind.

- **Incorporate Affirmations:** As you visualize your goals, silently repeat affirmations that align with the images on your board. These affirmations should specifically counter any limiting beliefs you've identified, helping you to build new, positive mental pathways. For example, if your board includes images related to health and wellness, you might repeat affirmations like, "I am healthy, strong, and full of energy." Combining visualization with affirmations reinforces the positive beliefs and emotions associated with your goals.

- **Reflect on Your Progress:** At the end of each day, take a moment to reflect on your progress toward your goals. Consider not only the steps you've taken but also how you've overcome any mental or emotional blocks that arose. Look at your vision board and consider what actions you took that day to move closer to your aspirations. Celebrate your small wins and remind yourself that each step, no matter how small, brings you closer to the life you envision.

- **Update Your Vision Board Regularly:** As you achieve your goals or your aspirations evolve, update your vision board to reflect your current desires. This process of updating also allows you to reassess any new neuroblocks that might have surfaced, ensuring that your vision board remains a relevant and powerful tool in your journey. Don't be afraid to remove images that no longer resonate with you or add new ones that inspire you. Your vision board should be a dynamic tool that grows and changes as you do.

As I mentioned previously, I started my vision journal around 2019, simply by writing everything I wanted to accomplish, no matter how large or small. What was most important was recognizing the neuroblocks that surfaced as I reflected on my goals and using my vision board to work through them. And check off what you accomplished. Being able to check off accomplishments motivated me to add more to my list and think delusionally to dream bigger.

Use Your Vision Board to Overcome Blocks
Whenever you encounter a block or challenge, turn to your vision board for inspiration. Look at the

images and words that represent your goals and remind yourself of why you're pursuing them. Use this time to visualize yourself overcoming a specific block, replacing it with empowering beliefs and actions. We all have setback days when we think the goal is bigger than ourselves. Visualize yourself overcoming the challenge and moving forward with confidence. Your vision board can serve as a powerful motivator during difficult times, helping you stay focused and committed to your path.

The Impact of Vision Boards on Motivation and Success

The use of vision boards has been supported by both anecdotal evidence and psychological research. A study conducted by Dr. Gail Matthews, a psychology professor at Dominican University in California, found that people who wrote their goals, shared them with others, and sent weekly updates to a friend were significantly more likely to achieve their goals than those who kept their goals to themselves.[31] By integrating the practice of recognizing and addressing neuroblocks with the use of vision boards, you can enhance this process even further, making your journey toward success more focused and resilient. Vision boards can enhance this process by providing a visual and tangible representation of your goals, which helps to reinforce your commitment and keep you motivated.

For me, adding images to the list, such as saving videos on my social media that represent what my future state of owning an internationally renowned gallery like the Louvre looked like, was helpful to motivate me. It also helped me identify and work through the subconscious beliefs that might have otherwise sabotaged my success. I started following designers, architects, fellow artists, and real estate leaders to build my algorithm to align with where I was going, not who I was previously. This goal is not fully completed but ingrained in my current actions as of early 2024, but I know everything in my timeline will take me closer to my vision to give back and help others through my and others' art.

Vision boards tap into the power of the Reticular Activating System (RAS), a part of the brain that filters information and influences what you focus on. By regularly looking at your vision board, you program your RAS to prioritize the goals and aspirations depicted on the board. This process also helps in filtering out the negative thoughts and beliefs that contribute to your neuroblocks, allowing you to focus more effectively on your goals. This heightened focus can lead to increased awareness of opportunities and resources that align with your goals, making it easier to take the necessary steps to achieve them.[32]

The Transformative Power of Visualization and Vision Boards

Years ago, Steve Harvey sparked my journey with vision boards. He said, "You have to see it before you can receive it. If you can see it in your mind, you can hold it in your hand."[33] Harvey's belief in the power of visualization through vision boards resonated deeply with me. His words encouraged me to visualize my goals and aspirations not just as distant dreams, but as tangible realities that I could work toward every day

Visualization, combined with a vision board, is more than just a mental exercise; it's a powerful tool that can transform how you approach and overcome the blocks in your life. By vividly imagining yourself achieving your goals and overcoming the specific challenges that hinder your progress, you can reprogram your mind to navigate these obstacles with greater confidence and ease. Whether dealing with fear, procrastination, or self-doubt, visualization, and vision boards provide a proactive way to break through these barriers and move closer to your goals every day.

Incorporating visualization and a vision board into your daily routine empowers you to take control of your narrative, shifting from a mindset of limitation to one of possibility. As you consistently engage in this practice, you'll find that the neuroblocks that once seemed insurmountable dissipate, replaced by a clear and focused path toward your goals. With each visualization session and every glance at your vision board, you are not just imagining a better future—you are actively creating it.

CHAPTER 6

Setting Goals So High You Sound Delusional

Setting Goals So High You Sound Delusional

The Art of Delusional-Level Goal Setting

Imagine having a vision so bold that it makes you question your own sanity—a vision so audacious that when you voice it, others can't help but raise an eyebrow. If you've never experienced this, it might be time to stretch your imagination further. Setting goals that seem unattainable is a craft in itself. These goals demand that you expand your thinking, confront your limitations, and evolve into a version of yourself you never thought possible.

But why aim for the seemingly impossible? Why set goals that appear to be so large and out of reach? The answer is simple: because these are the goals that will transform your life. When you set goals that stretch your imagination, you open yourself up to new possibilities and force yourself to think creatively. You break free from the constraints of your current reality and see the world as a place of infinite potential.

Delusional-level goal setting is not about being reckless or unrealistic. It's about tapping into the power of visionary thinking—the ability to imagine a future that is radically different and better than the present. It's about embracing the idea that the only limits are the ones you impose on yourself. And most importantly, it's about taking action to make those wild dreams a reality.

I spent my summers from the age of 12 working with my Grandpa Jamison, who founded a tool and die-making manufacturing company early in life. Grandpa would always say, "There is a right way, a wrong way, and Grandpa's way, which is always right!" It didn't dawn on me until recently that what he meant was that he was always on the path to success, even when there were bumps in the road. Grandpa took a long time to complete college, but he did it. He was trying to teach me not to give up, to go for it anyway. My oldest son is named after Grandpa because he had such a significant impact on my life—he taught me to go for it, even when people looked at me like I was nuts. To this day, when I tell someone an idea, and they respond with, "Wow, that is quite the goal," and raise an eyebrow, I smirk and say, "I know," and then go do it anyway!

Transitioning from the military to a full-time career as an artist wasn't something that happened overnight. It was a process that required setting delusional DUMB goals, pushing through self-doubt, and taking massive action to make my dreams a reality. It was about embracing the idea that I could create a life that combined my passion for art with my need for financial stability and fulfillment.

In this chapter, we'll walk through a detailed, step-by-step blueprint of how to set goals so high that they seem impossible. These steps will help you tap into your inner child's sense of wonder and possibility, visualize your success, and set goals that push you far beyond your comfort zone. By the end of this chapter, you'll be armed with the tools you need to dream bigger than ever before and take the first steps toward making those dreams come true.

To get the most out of these exercises, download the DUMB Goals Workbook PDF. thejuliejamison.com/DUMBGoalsWorkbook

Step 1: Acting Like Your Five-Year-Old Self—The Daydreaming Exercise

One of the best ways to tap into your creativity and set delusional-level DUMB goals is to act like your five-year-old self. Remember when you were a child and everything seemed possible? You could be a superhero, a movie star, a world traveler—all in the same day. Children have an innate sense of wonder and possibility that often gets lost as they grow older.

The Daydreaming Exercise

1. **Find a Quiet Space:** Start by finding a quiet space where you won't be disturbed. This could be a cozy corner of your home, a

peaceful spot in nature, or even a quiet room with soft music playing in the background.

2. **Close Your Eyes:** Close your eyes and take a few deep breaths. Allow yourself to relax and let go of any tension or stress.

3. **Imagine You're Five Years Old Again:** You have no responsibilities, limitations, or fear. The world is your playground, and you can do anything you want.

4. **Start Daydreaming:** Allow your mind to wander and daydream about your future. What do you want to be when you grow up? Where do you want to go? What adventures do you want to have? Let your imagination run wild, and don't hold back.

5. **Write Your Daydreams:** After you've spent some time daydreaming, open your eyes and write everything you imagined. Don't worry about whether it's realistic or not—just capture the essence of your dreams.

This exercise is a powerful way to reconnect with your inner child and tap into the limitless possibilities of your imagination. By allowing yourself to dream like a five-year-old, you can set goals that are truly inspiring and life-changing.

For me, reconnecting with my inner child meant allowing myself to dream of a life where I could fully embrace my creativity without limitations. It meant giving myself permission to pursue my passion for art, even if it seemed impractical or unrealistic at first. By tapping into that childlike sense of wonder, I was able to set goals that pushed me to grow and evolve in ways I never thought possible.

Step 2: Visualization Exercise—Turning Dreams into Reality

Now that you've tapped into your inner child and daydreamed about your wildest dreams, it's time to take those dreams and start turning them into reality. Visualization is a powerful tool for achieving your goals. By spending time each day visualizing yourself living your dream life, you can align your thoughts, emotions, and actions with your vision.

Visualization Exercise

1. **Review Your Daydreams:** Look at the list of daydreams you wrote in Step 1. Pick one or two that resonate with you the most.

2. **Visualize Success:** Spend a few minutes each day visualizing yourself achieving these dreams. Imagine every detail discussed in Chapter 5—how it feels, what you see, who is with you, and what your life looks like once you've achieved these goals. Visualization

taps into your subconscious mind, helping you believe your goals are attainable.

3. For example, I visualized myself as a successful artist, running a thriving business and making a meaningful impact through my work. I imagined what it would feel like to see my art in galleries, to collaborate with other creative minds, and to inspire others to pursue their passions. Many people attribute success to money, as did I before I realized money is only one facet of the journey. My initial success was allowing myself to be in my creative space daily. I saw a shift in my family within only two months. My older children were embracing their creativity as if they were 5-year-old children again. I was so grateful I could show them through my actions you can absolutely be successful in pursuing your love in life, whether it is becoming an artist, a full stay-at-home parent, or president of the United States. The small wins sometimes feel bigger than the large ones.

4. **Write Your Observations:** As you visualize, note any thoughts, feelings, or insights that arise. Write them down without judgment. This will help you gain clarity and deepen your connection to your goals.

5. Revisit Your Visualization Regularly: Make visualization a part of your daily routine. The more consistently you visualize your success, the more real it will become in your mind.

Visualization isn't just about wishful thinking; it's rooted in cognitive psychology. The brain doesn't always differentiate between vividly imagined scenarios and real-life experiences.[34] Regularly visualizing yourself achieving your goals creates new neural pathways that make success more likely.

When I first started stepping foot outside daily to go for walks or hikes, I would visualize the paths connecting in my mind, even when they seemed steep or unfamiliar. This exercise allowed me to trust my instincts, much like when I ventured into new territories in my career. Visualization empowered me to face challenges with confidence and a sense of adventure, knowing that my mind was already primed for success.

Step 3: Setting Delusional & Uncomfortable Goals—The Five Whys Method

Now that you've reconnected with your inner child and visualized your success, it's time to set your goals. But not just any goals—delusional and uncomfortable goals that push you beyond your limits and force you to grow.

Identifying Comfortable and Uncomfortable Goals

1. **Review Your Visualization Observations:** Look at the notes you made during your visualization exercise. Identify which goals feel comfortable and which ones feel uncomfortable or even delusional.

2. **Write Your Goals:** Start by writing your comfortable goals—those that feel within reach but still require effort. Then, write your uncomfortable goals—those that feel challenging, scary, or even impossible.

3. **Apply the Five Whys Method:** For each uncomfortable goal, ask yourself, *Why?* five times. This technique helps you dig deep and uncover the root motivation behind your goals. It also helps you identify any potential roadblocks or fears holding you back. Here is an example of the Five Whys Method:

   • **Goal:** I want to build a multi-million-dollar art business.

     ○ **Why?** Because I want to provide a better life for my family and give back to the community through service.

- ○ **Why?** Because I want my children and those in our community to have opportunities I didn't have.

- ○ **Why?** Because I want financial freedom.

- ○ **Why?** Because I believe I have the power to create generational wealth and change my family's future.

- ○ **Why?** Because I want to own my time and feel I can do whatever I want for myself and my family.

By the end of this exercise, you'll have a list of delusional and uncomfortable goals rooted in your deepest motivations. These goals will challenge you, push you out of your comfort zone, and ultimately transform your life.

Building Accountability and Moving Forward

Once you've set your delusional and uncomfortable goals, the next step is to build accountability and start taking action. This process involves setting deadlines, creating a support network, and taking consistent steps toward your goals.

1. **Set a Deadline:** A goal without a deadline is just a wish. Set a deadline for each goal, even if it feels unrealistic. The deadline will create a sense of urgency and motivate you

to take action. I set deadlines for myself, such as launching my 1 of 1 Fine Art collection by a certain date (less than one month) or reaching a specific revenue target within the first year of business. These deadlines helped keep me focused and motivated, even when the journey seemed daunting. However, I adjusted as I learned more about the industry.

2. **Create a Support Network:** Surround yourself with people who believe in your vision and will hold you accountable. This could be a mentor, a friend, or a community of like-minded individuals. Their support and encouragement will help you stay on track. My husband, friends, and mentors all played a crucial role in helping me stay focused and motivated. They provided the encouragement I needed to keep going, even when I faced challenges or setbacks.

3. **Take Consistent Action:** Start taking massive action toward your goals. Don't wait for the perfect moment—start now, even if you're not fully prepared. Remember, the journey of a thousand miles begins with a single step. The key is to keep moving forward, no matter how small the steps seem. I took massive action by dedicating time each

day to working on my art, building my business, and developing new skills. I reached out to potential clients and collaborators, invested in the tools and resources I needed, and pushed myself to step far outside of my comfort zone.

Overcoming Challenges and Staying Motivated

Pursuing delusional and uncomfortable goals comes with its challenges. Sometimes you encounter obstacles, face setbacks, or question whether you're on the right path. In these moments, staying motivated and pushing forward is essential.

1. **Practice Resilience:** Success rarely comes overnight—it's the result of consistent effort and a willingness to keep going, even when the going gets tough. Resilience is about bouncing back from setbacks and using them as learning opportunities. Throughout my journey, I faced self-doubt and challenges that seemed insurmountable. But I reminded myself of the lessons my Grandpa Jamison taught me—to keep going, even when others think you're crazy, and to trust that you're on the success path, even when there are bumps in the road.

2. Celebrate Small Wins: Take time to acknowledge your achievements, no matter how small, and use them as fuel to keep moving forward. Every step you take brings you closer to your goal, and each victory, no matter how minor, is a testament to your determination and resilience. I celebrated every milestone, from launching my first art collection to securing my first client. These small wins motivated me and reminded me of how far I had come.

3. Reflect and Adjust: As you work toward your goals, reflect on your progress and adjust as needed. Are you on track to achieve your goals? Are there any obstacles that you need to overcome? Use this reflection time to stay focused and motivated and be willing to adjust your plan if necessary. I regularly reflected on my progress, celebrated my successes, and learned from my setbacks. I adjusted my goals and strategies as needed, always keeping my ultimate vision in mind.

The Journey of a Delusional Goal Setter

Setting goals so high you sound like your delusional is not for the faint of heart. It requires courage, creativity, and a willingness to step into the uncomfortable zone. But the rewards are worth it.

When you set goals that stretch your imagination and push you to grow, you open yourself up to new possibilities and create a life that is truly extraordinary.

As you embark on this journey, remember that it's not just about achieving specific milestones—it's about the person you become along the way. It's about building a life that aligns with your deepest values and passions, and it's about creating a legacy that will inspire others to dream big and pursue their own delusional-level goals.

So go ahead—set goals that seem impossible, take massive action to achieve them, and trust that you have the power to make your wildest dreams a reality. And when others look at you like you're crazy, just smirk and go do it anyway.

CHAPTER 7

Moving Out on Your Goals and Removing Neuroblocks

Moving Out On Your Goals and Removing Neuroblocks

The Importance of Taking Action

In the previous chapter, we explored the power of setting delusional-level DUMB goals—goals so big that they stretch your imagination, challenge everything you know, and push you to embrace being comfortable with discomfort. But setting goals is only the first step. The real transformation happens when you start taking action to make those goals a reality while simultaneously recognizing that discomfort is part of the process. As Zig Ziglar famously said, "You don't have to be great to start, but you have to start to be great."[35]

This chapter is about moving out on your goals, one step at a time. It's about breaking down your big, audacious goals into manageable steps and taking consistent action every day. Along the way, we'll discuss how to remove any remaining neuroblocks holding you back, how to stay motivated and focused on your journey, and how to effectively map out your 30-day, 90-day, 6-month, 1-year, and 2-5-year plans. We'll move out on your goals while simultaneously removing any blocks that may arise along the way.

Breaking Down Your Goals into Actionable Steps

Once you've set your delusional-level DUMB goals, the next step is to break them down into actionable steps. This is where many people get stuck—they have big dreams but don't know how to turn them into reality. If you have not done so by now, please gather a designated journal, open a Word document, or notes on your phone to accomplish the exercises in this chapter. If at any time this feels like a lot, walk away for five minutes and come back. Remember, we are going to the uncomfortable zone, you will eventually become accustomed to being uncomfortable as you take action to pursue our dreams. I highly recommend not stepping away for over five minutes, as you will find something to distract you and not accomplish the exercise.

Let's go...

Step 1: Identify the Key Milestones

Before transitioning from the military to corporate leadership and eventually becoming a full-time artist and entrepreneur, I set an audacious goal that mentally and physically challenged me. I decided to earn my project management certification, giving myself only four months to prepare for the test—a delusional goal considering the complexity of the material and the circumstances. At the time, I was pregnant with my fourth child and preparing for maternity leave. COVID restrictions meant I had to take the test at home, under strict supervision, with no papers, pens, or anyone else in the room.

On the day of the test, I was eight months pregnant and feeling incredibly sick. Unbeknownst to me, I found out a few days later I had contracted COVID, which explained why I felt so terrible. The stakes were high—I had invested over $500 in the test and countless hours of courses and studying, and the pressure of passing while feeling unprepared weighed heavily on me. Before my husband left that morning, I told him I did not feel confident going into my test. Most likely from lingering test anxiety from my early ROTC days. He gave me his traditional "Dad advice" before leaving: "The key to passing the test is answering the questions correctly." I laughed, telling him to get out so I could focus, despite the nerves gnawing at me.

The test took nearly four hours, during which I tried not to move too much or sneeze, as any suspicious movement could cause the termination of my test. When I finished and saw the words "Congratulations...Pass" on the screen, I could hardly believe it. I passed on the first try, and not only that, but I also scored exceptionally high. I read the results on the screen at least 50 times because the font was small, and my brain struggled to process the victory.

Sometimes, life surprises you when you set a clear blueprint for your success. I remember telling myself that I had no choice but to pass the days leading up— after all, the baby could arrive any day, and taking a test sleep-deprived was not an option. My mental programming worked, reminding me of the power of setting ambitious milestones and sticking to them, even when the odds seem stacked against you.

Identifying key milestones is the first step in turning your big, delusional-level DUMB goals into a reality. Milestones are significant checkpoints or goals within your larger plan.

Exercise: Defining Your Key Milestones

To help you identify your key milestones, consider the following steps and questions:

- **Envision Your End Goal**

  What is your ultimate goal? What does success look like for you? Take a moment to visualize the end result of your efforts. Picture yourself at the finish line—what have you accomplished? What do you feel when you reach your goal? Visualize the emotions you experience upon reaching your goal. Are you feeling proud, relieved, excited, or perhaps fulfilled? Understanding the emotional payoff can help motivate you throughout your journey. **Example:** If your goal is to start a billion-dollar company, envision what that looks like. Are you leading a large team? Are you changing an industry? What specific outcomes do you see? What emotions come to the surface as you visualize achieving this goal?

- **Break Down Your Big Picture Vision**

  Think about the major components that must be achieved to reach your end goal. What are the broad categories of tasks or projects that need to be completed?

  Example: For a billion-dollar company, the broad categories might include creating a groundbreaking product or service, securing significant investments if required, and scaling operations locally or globally.

- **Identify Critical Milestones**

  Within each broad category, identify specific milestones that signify major progress. What are the key achievements that will indicate you are on track?

  Example: If creating a groundbreaking product is a category, critical milestones could include completing the initial prototype, securing patents, and receiving positive feedback from early testers.

- **Sequence Your Milestones**

  Consider the order in which these milestones need to be achieved. What needs to happen first, second, and so on? Sequence them logically to create a roadmap. You may not know every milestone but write what you see and know is required as of today, and fill in the remaining as you go forward.

  Example: Before you can secure investment, you may need to complete your business plan and prototype. Sequence your milestones accordingly.

- **Set Milestones That Challenge You**

  Ensure that your milestones are ambitious enough to push you into the uncomfortable zone in a good way. Are these milestones stretching your abilities and resources?

  Example: Set a milestone to secure funding within six months, even if it feels challenging. This will push you to move quickly and stay focused.

By following these steps and asking these questions, you can break down your big, delusional-level DUMB goals into key, challenging, and achievable milestones. These milestones will serve as your roadmap, guiding you on your journey and providing clear indicators of progress along the way.

Step 2: Break Down Each Milestone

Once you've identified your key milestones, it's time to break each one down into smaller, actionable steps. This process will make your larger goals more manageable and help you stay on track.

For instance, if one of your milestones is to develop a business plan, you can break it down into smaller tasks such as researching your market, defining your target audience, and outlining your revenue model. Each step is a building block toward your larger goal.

In my journey, breaking down milestones meant developing a concrete blueprint for each phase of my business. For example, when I set the goal of launching my first art collection, I broke it down into tasks like selecting the theme, creating the pieces, marketing, and setting up a launch event. Each step was a move toward the larger goal, making the entire process less overwhelming. Remember, no one knows what they are doing till they try!

Exercise: Breaking Down Your Milestones

Here are some questions to guide you through breaking down your milestones:

- **What is the main milestone you want to achieve?**

  Start by clearly defining the milestone. For example:

  - *Launching an online course:* "I want to launch a successful online course in six months."

  - *Writing a book:* "I want to finish writing my first novel in nine months."

  - *Starting a business:* "I want to launch my e-commerce business by the end of the year."

  - *Health and fitness:* "I want to run a marathon in 12 months."

  - *Artistic achievement:* "I want to complete a solo art exhibition in eight months."

- **What are the smaller tasks required to achieve this milestone?**

  Break down the milestone into specific tasks. For example:

  - *Launching an online course:*

    - Researching course topics and audience needs.

- Outlining the course curriculum.
- Recording and editing course videos.
- Creating supplementary materials (e.g., worksheets, quizzes).
- Setting up the course on an online platform.
- Marketing the course to your target audience.

o *Writing a book:*

- Developing the book's plot and characters.
- Creating a writing schedule.
- Writing the first draft, chapter by chapter.
- Revising and editing the manuscript.
- Finding a publisher or self-publishing.
- Planning the book launch and marketing strategy.

o *Starting a business:*

- Conducting market research to validate your business idea.
- Creating a business plan with financial projections.
- Sourcing suppliers or developing your product/service.

- Building a website and setting up social media channels.
- Registering your business and securing necessary permits.
- Launching a marketing campaign to attract your first customers.

○ *Health and fitness:*

- Researching a marathon training plan.
- Scheduling regular runs and strength training sessions.
- Joining a running group or finding a training partner.
- Tracking your progress and adjusting your plan as needed.
- Registering for the marathon and planning race-day logistics.

○ *Artistic Achievement:*

- Deciding on the theme and concept for your exhibition.
- Creating a timeline for completing each artwork.
- Securing a venue for the exhibition.
- Planning the layout and presentation of your art.
- Marketing the exhibition to attract attendees.

➤ Coordinating with galleries or sponsors for support.

- **What resources or skills do you need for each task?**

  Identify any resources or skills you need to complete each task. For instance:

  ○ *Launching an online course:*
    ➤ Learning video editing software.
    ➤ Hiring a graphic designer for course materials.
    ➤ Investing in a good microphone and camera for recording.

  ○ *Writing a book:*
    ➤ Start putting your ideas on paper. Write, just write!
    ➤ Finding a professional editor or critique partner.
    ➤ Researching literary agents or self-publishing platforms.

  ○ *Starting a business:*
    ➤ Learning about e-commerce platforms.
    ➤ Hiring a web developer or using a website builder.
    ➤ Taking a course on digital marketing.

○ *Health and Fitness:*

  ➤ Consulting with a personal trainer or coach.

  ➤ Investing in quality running shoes and gear.

  ➤ Using a fitness tracker or app to monitor progress.

○ *Artistic Achievement:*

  ➤ Purchasing high-quality art supplies.

  ➤ Learning new techniques or taking an art class.

  ➤ Networking with other artists and curators.

- **What are potential obstacles, and how can you overcome them?**

  Consider any challenges that might arise and plan how to address them. For example:

  ○ *Launching an online course:*

    ➤ Obstacle: Lack of time to create content.

    ➤ Solution: Schedule dedicated content creation days each week.

  ○ *Writing a book:*

    ➤ Obstacle: Writer's block or lack of inspiration.

- ➤ Solution: Set a daily writing goal and create a routine to spark creativity.
  - ○ *Starting a business:*
    - ➤ Obstacle: Difficulty securing funding.
    - ➤ Solution: Explore alternative funding options like crowdfunding or small business grants.
  - ○ *Health and Fitness:*
    - ➤ Obstacle: Risk of injury during training.
    - ➤ Solution: Include rest days and cross-training to prevent overuse injuries.
  - ○ *Artistic achievement:*
    - ➤ Obstacle: Finding a venue or sponsorship for the exhibition.
    - ➤ Solution: Start networking early and explore alternative spaces like pop-up galleries.

- **How can you measure progress for each task?**

  Determine how you will track your progress. For example:
  - ○ *Launching an online course:*
    - ➤ Set deadlines for completing each module of the course.

- ➤ Track the number of sign-ups or pre-enrollments.
- ○ *Writing a book:*
  - ➤ Set word count or chapter goals for each day/week.
  - ➤ Track completion of each chapter or section.
- ○ *Starting a business:*
  - ➤ Monitor progress on tasks like website launch, product development, and marketing campaigns.
  - ➤ Track key performance indicators (KPIs) like customer acquisition and sales.
- ○ *Health and Fitness:*
  - ➤ Track your running distance, pace, and endurance over time.
  - ➤ Monitor improvements in strength and flexibility.
- ○ *Artistic achievement:*
  - ➤ Track the completion of each artwork.
  - ➤ Monitor engagement and interest in the exhibition through social media and RSVPs.

Step 3: Create a Timeline

Next, create a timeline for achieving each of your milestones. Be realistic about how long each step will take, but also push yourself to move quickly. Remember, the goal is to create a sense of urgency and momentum. This is where the importance of spelling out your 30-day, 90-day, 6-month, 1-year, and 2-5-year plans comes into play.

When I expanded my business plan in the middle of 2024, I wrote down as much detail as I could. This included when and who I wanted to hire down to the order in which I would bring contractors onto my team. After coming out of the Hamptons Fine Art Fair, I planned when I would increase my art to a six-figure price point for my day-to-day galleries and other key milestones. But I didn't stop there. I looked at this plan and asked myself, *Why would I wait to increase the price of my art? Why would I do it now? Or should I wait? What are the internal and external reasons I would wait?*

After discussing it with my husband, we talked through two price points that were my next possible increases. We discussed the numbers I was comfortable with, and I went for the one over the six-figure mark. For some reason, the six-figure price didn't bother me as much as the higher five-figure amount. You might ask why? It's because I recognized my value. The six-figure price aligned more with the worth I saw in myself and my work.

Mel Robbins, a renowned motivational speaker, has a technique that resonated with me during this process. She talks about how she was taught to sit in the moment and say, "I usually charge double," then be silent when negotiating her speaking engagement commissions. It's not about the money; it's about knowing what your time on this earth is worth. For me, this principle applied to my art. I had to recognize that my work and my time were valuable and that I deserved to set prices that reflected that value. I would rather live under a bridge than partner with someone who does not align with my core values of people first, service, and integrity in my decision-making.

Exercise: As You Create Your Timeline

Challenge yourself with the following questions to ensure you're not just setting realistic timelines, but also pushing yourself to achieve your milestones faster:

- **What is your 30-day plan?**
    - Which milestones can you realistically achieve in the next 30 days?
    - What specific tasks must be completed within the first week to establish a strong foundation?

- ○ Who do you need to contact or network with to make progress immediately?
- ○ What resources or tools do you need to gather or prepare in the next 30 days?
- ○ Why am I giving myself 30 days for this task? Can I realistically complete it in a week or two?
- ○ Is this timeline based on external factors, or is it because of an internal block such as fear or procrastination?
- ○ What steps can you automate, delegate, or streamline to achieve this milestone faster?
- ○ How will you measure your success at the end of this 30-day period?

- **What is your 90-day plan?**
  - ○ What larger milestones should you accomplish within the next three months?
  - ○ How can you break these milestones into weekly or bi-weekly tasks to maintain momentum?
  - ○ Are there any dependencies or prerequisites for achieving these milestones, and how can you address them in advance?
  - ○ Can you combine certain tasks or streamline processes to shorten the 90-day timeline?

○ Why are you setting this milestone for 90 days? Could you realistically achieve it in 60 days?

● **What is your 6-month plan?**

○ What major milestones do you expect to achieve within six months?

○ Are there any skills, knowledge, or resources you need to acquire to hit these milestones?

○ What partnerships or collaborations could accelerate your progress?

○ Can you set interim milestones every two months to stay on track and avoid last-minute pressure?

○ What is preventing you from reaching this milestone sooner? Is it a practical limitation, or could it be an internal block?

● **What is your 1-year plan?**

○ What are the critical milestones you need to achieve by the end of the year?

○ How will your 6-month achievements build toward these 1-year goals?

○ What long-term preparations do you need to make now to ensure success by the 12-month mark?

- ○ Could any of these milestones be achieved earlier with more focused effort or by eliminating distractions?
- ○ Why am I setting a full year to achieve this goal? Is this timeline necessary, or can I shrink it?

- **What is your 2-5 year plan?**
  - ○ What are the key long-term milestones that will define your success over the next 2-5 years?
  - ○ How do your 1-year goals set the stage for these longer-term objectives?
  - ○ Are there any major shifts or pivots you anticipate, and how can you plan for them now?
  - ○ Can you identify potential obstacles or bottlenecks that could slow your progress, and how can you address them proactively?
  - ○ What would happen if you aimed to achieve these 2-5 year goals in 1-2 years instead? What would need to change to make that possible?

Step 4: Shrinking the Timeline

As you break down your milestones into smaller tasks, it's essential to ask yourself if the timeframes you've set are realistic or if they can be accelerated. The 80/20 rule, originally introduced by Vilfredo Pareto in the early 20th century, suggests that 80% of results come from 20% of efforts or inputs.[36] In decision-making, this principle encourages focusing on the most impactful actions or decisions that drive most outcomes, rather than waiting for perfection. This principle has been further popularized and adapted for modern business strategies by authors like Richard Koch.[37] By aligning this with the idea of "80% on a decision and move out, you're reminded that waiting for 100% certainty before acting can lead to stagnation or missed opportunities. Instead, once you're about 80% confident in a decision, it's better to take action and adjust as needed along the way.

This idea ties directly into the mindset to move at the speed of excellence. Excellence doesn't require perfection; it's about consistently pushing forward with growth in mind, even when you've reached a high standard. I often heard this phrase early in military training, and it taught me that improvement is a continuous process.[38] Even when you think you've mastered something, the question becomes, "What can I do to be better?" By focusing on the 20% of key actions that drive the most results,[39] and by moving forward decisively, you can maintain momentum while still pursuing excellence. This directly relates to shrinking your timeline. Perfection is not what I want you to aim for. I would like you to know 80% good is more than enough to press forward allowing you to shrink timelines in the accomplishment of your goals.

Exercise: Assess Your Speed of Excellence

- **Can you accomplish this task faster, effectively, and efficiently?**

  o Question the timeline you've set. If you think a task will take a month, ask yourself, *Could I complete it in two weeks or less? Why am I waiting until this point to accomplish this goal?* Challenge all the assumptions that are slowing you down.

- **Is there an internal block causing delays?**

  Reflect on whether internal blocks, such as fear of failure or perfectionism, are causing you to set longer timelines. Address these blocks head-on by reminding yourself of your capabilities and the importance of pushing into the uncomfortable zone. If you are telling yourself it takes 90 days, it will take 90 days. When you know you only have two weeks to accomplish a task, you accomplish what you can best in two weeks. This is not to say it will be a perfect result, but what it does is remove the safety net of your comfort zone.

- **Use the Five Whys Technique:**

  When you identify an internal block, take a deep breath and ask yourself the "5 Whys" to get to the root of the issue:

  - Why am I hesitating to take action?
  - Why does this particular task make me uncomfortable?
  - Why do I feel unprepared or inadequate?
  - Why am I afraid of the potential outcome?
  - Why do I believe this might lead to failure?

- **Are there external factors slowing you down that you can control or influence?**

  - Determine if the delay is due to external factors (e.g., waiting on someone else).
  - Identify any external factors that might be affecting your timeline. For instance, if you're waiting for feedback from others, can you follow up sooner or find alternative ways to proceed?
  - Do not feel you are bugging others when you send one email or make a follow-up phone call.

○ Control what you can control, push where feels right, know you can only control you and your reactions to create your path.

By breaking down your milestones into smaller tasks and continuously challenging yourself to work efficiently, you'll create momentum and make steady progress toward your delusional-level goals.

Step 5: Take Daily Action

The concept of taking one step at a time is deeply rooted in the work of successful therapists and coaches. For example, Dr. Albert Ellis, the founder of Rational Emotive Behavior Therapy (REBT), emphasized the importance of taking small, consistent actions to overcome psychological barriers and achieve personal goals.[40] In my own life, taking daily action meant consistently creating art, networking, and refining my business strategy, no matter how busy or overwhelmed I felt.

For example, I continue to this day to go hiking with my camera gear. Why? Because I need my camera to be an extension of my body like muscle memory when I am on my larger scheduled shoots. Even if I never release the photographs, the goal is to be better and better at my craft every day. I love photographing animals, but they, like having four young children, tend to move a lot when you are trying to catch an action shot. When time allows, I head to nature realms where I know smaller wildlife is to catch action shots and train myself to be faster while completely aware of my surroundings. My goal is to take photographs of bears, moose, and more up in Alaska and on international trips and safaris.

Exercise: Take AIM

Taking consistent daily action is crucial in moving closer to your delusional-level DUMB goals. To ensure you're making progress every day, follow my AIM method: Action, Improve, Motivate. This structured approach will help you maintain focus, overcome obstacles, and continuously refine your efforts. Here's how to apply the Take AIM exercise:

- **Action: What is the one thing I can do today to move closer to my goal?**

  Start your day with a clear objective. As soon as you begin your day, ask yourself, *What is the most important action I can take today that will advance me toward my goal?* This works even better when you plan your day the night before. Do all actions lead to your one step for the day? Before you know it, you will manage multiple steps in one day to make large strides toward your goal.

Example Questions:

- ○ What small step can I take today that will push my project forward?

- ○ Is there a critical email or call that needs to be made?

- ○ Can I dedicate time to work on a specific task that will have a significant impact? Daily Practice: Write down the one action you commit to taking today. Keep it visible throughout the day (e.g., on a sticky note or in your planner). This practice aligns with the "small wins" concept in psychology, which emphasizes the power of incremental progress in achieving larger goals.[41]

- **Improve:** How can I overcome today's biggest obstacle?

  Identify and tackle your biggest challenge: During your day, reflect on the obstacles that could prevent you from completing your key action. Address these challenges directly. The phrase "slay your dragons early in the day" is often attributed to Brian Tracy, a motivational speaker and author.[42] He popularized the idea in his book *Eat That Frog!*, which emphasizes tackling your most challenging tasks first thing in the morning. This concept aligns with

the idea of "slaying your dragons" or addressing your biggest obstacles early in the day to
set a productive tone for the rest of your day.

Example Questions:

- ○ What is the biggest hurdle (i.e., your
  dragon) I face today in achieving my goal?
- ○ Do I need more resources, time, or motivation to overcome this obstacle?
- ○ How can I break down this challenge into
  manageable parts?

Daily Practice:

As challenges arise, write your primary
obstacle and brainstorm one or two strategies to overcome it. Implement those
strategies immediately. This approach is
rooted in Cognitive Behavioral Therapy
(CBT), which encourages active problem-
solving to reduce psychological barriers.[43]

- **Motivate:** What can I do better tomorrow
  based on today's progress?

End your day with reflection and improvement: At the close of your day, evaluate what
you've achieved and think about how you can
improve tomorrow.

Coming from nuclear operations, we com-
monly "debriefed" after any training session

or alert. The purpose of the debrief was to analyze and evaluate what happened during the mission, identify what went well, and determine areas for improvement. This process involves gathering information from all participants, discussing the execution of the mission, and addressing any deviations from the plan. The goal is to learn from the experience, improve future performance, and ensure that any lessons learned are communicated effectively across the unit or organization. Long story short, "debriefs" are meant to motivate individuals to strive to be better every day. Even when you feel everything was so-called "perfect," there is usually at least one area of improvement that could adjust your entire blueprint to faster success.

Example Questions:

o Did I effectively complete the action/mission/objective I set out to do today?

o Was there anything that could have been done more efficiently or effectively?

o How can I apply the lessons I learned today to be more productive tomorrow?

Daily Practice:

Spend 5-10 minutes to prepare your next day's goals, then review today's actions.

Write one improvement you can make for the next day and how you'll implement it. This is not a time to beat yourself up for mistakes, but take an objective, outside perspective review of what you could do better.

AIM Exercise: Daily Routine

- **Morning:** Set and review your daily Action. Identify the one critical task that will push you closer to your goal.

  Write down your action. (Preferably the evening prior)

  Keep it in front of you all day.

- **Midday:** Reflect on Improvement. As you work, pinpoint today's biggest obstacle and find a way to overcome it.

  Write down the obstacle and your solution. Take immediate steps to implement your solution.

- **Evening:** Motivate yourself for tomorrow with your debrief. Review your day and identify one improvement for the next day.

  Reflect on today's success and challenges. Write down your improvement plan for tomorrow.

Recap of the AIM Exercise:

- Action: Start each day with a clear, impactful goal.
- Improve: Address and overcome obstacles as they arise.
- Motivate: Reflect on progress and plan for better efficiency the next day.

This exercise ensures you are always moving forward, refining your approach, and maintaining momentum in achieving your delusional-level goals. By incorporating the AIM method into your daily routine, you'll steadily make progress, even when the path is challenging.

Removing Neuroblocks Along the Way

As you move out on your goals, you may encounter neuroblocks—mental barriers that hold you back from taking action or achieving success. These can include fear of failure, self-doubt, perfectionism, or procrastination. In Chapter 5, we discussed how to identify and remove these blocks, but it's important to revisit this concept as you take action on your goals.

NASA's 1960s experiment to identify the creative genius in their engineers is a powerful example of this. They realized that children scored higher in creative thinking tests but lost this ability as they aged due to the rigid structures of education and societal expectations. The takeaway? It's never too late to regain that creativity, challenge your limiting beliefs, and start thinking like a genius again.[44]

Exercise: Removing Neuroblocks with the 3C Method

- **Step 1: Challenge Your Limiting Beliefs**
  - **Identify the Limiting Belief:**

    Pause and identify any limiting beliefs that have arisen throughout your day/week/month as you pursue your goals. Remember, this is an ongoing process that evolves with your journey.

    Write one specific limiting belief that has been holding you back.

  - **Question the Belief:**

    - What specific experiences or events led me to develop this belief? Reflect on the origin of the belief. Is it tied to a particular moment in your life, or has it developed gradually over time?

    - How would I view this belief if I were advising a friend? Imagine offering advice to someone else with the same belief. Would you encourage them to hold on to it, or would you challenge them to see things differently?

➤ What would happen if I let go of this belief? Consider the potential outcomes if you released this belief. How might it change your actions, mindset, or approach to your goals?

➤ Am I holding onto this belief out of habit or comfort? Explore whether the belief is something you've grown accustomed to, rather than something grounded in reality. Are you clinging to it because it feels familiar, even if it's not serving you?

➤ What alternative belief could better support my goals and growth? Think about a more empowering belief that could replace the limiting one. How would adopting this new belief change your perspective and progress?

○ **Replace the Belief:**

What alternative belief could better support my goals and growth? Think about a more empowering belief that could replace the limiting one. How would adopting this new belief change your perspective and progress? Write down a more empowering belief to replace the limiting one. Example: If your limiting belief is "I'm not creative enough," replace it with "I possess a distinct creative energy that I can access whenever I want."

- **Step 2: Convert Failures into Learning Opportunities**
  - ○ **Reflect on a Recent Failure:**

    Think about a recent failure or setback you've experienced on your journey. Write the details of this experience.

  - ○ **Extract the Lesson:**

    Ask yourself, *What can I learn from this experience?* Write at least one key lesson you've learned from the failure.

  - ○ **Plan Your Next Steps:**

    Consider how you can apply the lessons learned to future actions.

    Write the specific steps you will take to improve and move forward.

    Example: Should I adjust my social media presence since changing platforms? How long has it been since making the change? Is it best to wait two weeks/60 days to see if my original plan works?

- **Step 3: Continue with Self-Compassion**
  - **Acknowledge Your Progress:**

    Take a moment to recognize the progress you've made, even if things haven't gone perfectly.

    Write down at least one positive outcome or achievement from your recent efforts.

    Example: Maybe you come from years of not controlling how you react in a difficult situation. Maybe you would lose your temper and yell. But this time, you made great strides; your blood pressure did not rise, and you kept calm and handled the situation with grace. Celebrate how you handled your emotions!

  - **Practice Self-Compassion:**

    Ask yourself, *How can I be kinder to myself in this process?*

    Write a self-compassionate statement or affirmation that you can use when facing challenges.

    Example: Guilt is a real battle many individuals face daily. Since starting my business, I have been working every day to release guilt. I no longer allow myself to feel bad because I should do something more. I will do my best every day. After months of working seven days a week toward my goals, I allow myself to take a mental day off. Most of the time, I come back 100 times more focused and productive toward my goals.

○ **Support Your Well-Being:**

Consider what actions you can take to support your well-being while pursuing your goals. Write one or two specific self-care activities or practices you will implement. Remember: You are the only one that can take care of you!

Summary of the 3C Method

- Challenge your limiting beliefs by questioning their validity and replacing them with empowering thoughts.

- Convert failures into learning opportunities by reflecting on what went wrong and how to improve.

- Continue with self-compassion by acknowledging your progress, being kind to yourself, and supporting your well-being.

By following these steps regularly, you'll be better equipped to remove neuroblocks, maintain momentum, and achieve your delusional-level goals.

Seeking Feedback: Trusting Your Instincts and Your Inner Circle

When you're pursuing delusional-level DUMB goals, feedback is essential, but it's just as important to trust your instincts and the advice you'd give to a close friend in the same situation. This journey is deeply personal, and while guidance from others can be invaluable, your inner voice and intuition should lead the way.

Step 1: Identify Your Trusted Inner Circle

Your inner circle is not a large group—it's likely made up of just a few individuals, perhaps no more than 3-5 people. These are the people who match your high energy and high vibration—those who are on the same wavelength as you, with the same drive, positivity, and belief in limitless possibilities. High vibration refers to the energy you emit and absorb; it's about being in a state of joy, passion, and love, which attracts similar energy from others.

Questions to Ask Yourself:

- Who would I trust with my most ambitious dreams and deepest fears?
- Who consistently matches or elevates my energy and ambition?

- Who do I instinctively turn to when I need honest, no-nonsense feedback?
- Who would I give the same level of support and advice to if our roles were reversed?
- Who pushes me to go further, challenges me to be better, and believes in me without question?

Exercise: Write the names of those individuals who truly belong in your inner circle. Reflect on what makes each person uniquely valuable to your journey. These are the people you'll lean on when seeking feedback, knowing they will push you to be your best self while respecting your instincts.

Step 2: Trust Your Instincts and Your Inner Circle

As you gather feedback, remember that your instincts are just as crucial as the advice you receive. Sometimes, the best feedback you can give yourself is the kind you'd offer a trusted friend—kind, encouraging, and realistic.

Questions to Ask Yourself:

- What would I tell a friend if they were in my shoes right now?

- How does this feedback align with what I know to be true about myself and my goals?
- Am I feeling resistance to this feedback because it challenges me, or because it doesn't resonate with my true path?
- How does this feedback make me feel— energized and motivated, or doubtful and confused?

Exercise: After receiving feedback, take a moment to reflect on your gut reaction. Write down your initial thoughts and feelings. Then, ask yourself what advice you'd give to a friend in the same situation. Compare the two—often, you'll find clarity in aligning your instincts with the advice you'd offer someone you care about.

Step 3: Filter Feedback Through Your High Vibration Lens

Not all feedback will serve you, and that's okay. It's important to filter what you hear through your high-vibration lens—only absorbing what elevates you and discarding anything that brings you down or causes doubt without reason.

Questions to Ask Yourself:

- Does this feedback raise my energy and moti-vation, or does it lower my vibration?

- Is this advice coming from someone who understands and supports my vision?
- How does this feedback align with my long-term goals and the person I'm striving to become?
- Is this feedback something I would give to myself on my best day?

Exercise: Take time to filter through the feedback you've received, writing what resonates with you and what doesn't. Trust your high vibration to guide you in deciding what to keep and let go of. Remember, your path is unique, and not all advice will fit your journey.

Balancing Feedback with Instincts

In pursuing your delusional goals, trust is paramount—trust in your instincts, the feedback you'd give a friend, and the wisdom of your carefully chosen inner circle. These trusted voices should lift you, push you forward, and help you stay aligned with your highest energy and vibration. By keeping your circle small, selective, and filled with those who truly understand you, you'll navigate your path with confidence, knowing that the guidance you follow is in harmony with your deepest instincts.

CHAPTER 8

Tying It All Together—
Building Your Legacy

The Journey So Far

As we arrive at the final chapter of this book, it's time to reflect on the journey we've taken together. We've explored the power of visionary thinking, the importance of setting delusional-level goals, and the significance of taking consistent, determined action toward those goals. We've also discussed overcoming mental barriers, reprogramming your thinking, and staying motivated on your path to success.

It's time to tie everything together and focus on the bigger picture: building your legacy. Your legacy isn't just about what you achieve in your lifetime; it's about your impact on the world and the lives you touch. It's about creating something that will endure long after you're gone, inspiring future generations to dream big and pursue their goals.

Embracing Your Unique Journey

Each of us has a unique journey shaped by our experiences, challenges, and choices. My journey from military service to corporate leadership and eventually to becoming a full-time artist and entrepreneur has been anything but linear. It's been filled with twists and turns, successes and setbacks, and moments of doubt and clarity.

One of the most important lessons I've learned is that it's okay for your journey to differ from others. It should. Your journey is yours alone, and it's up to you to embrace it fully. Don't compare yourself to others or measure your success by their standards. Instead, focus on what makes you unique and how to use your gifts to make a difference in the world.

My journey has been guided by the lessons I learned from my grandparents. Grandpa Jamison, with his entrepreneurial spirit and unwavering determination, taught me the value of persistence and the importance of doing things your own way. Their legacy reminds me it's never too late to change, grow, and make a difference. Whether you're just starting out or well on your way, every step brings you closer to the person you're meant to become and the legacy you're meant to leave.

Are You Living Life, or Is Life Living You?

One of the most profound questions you can ask yourself is, "Are you living life, or is life living you?" This question cuts to the core of how we approach our days, decisions, and destinies. Too often, people drift through life, reacting to circumstances rather than creating their own path. They become spectators, watching from the sidelines as life passes them by.

But you have a choice. You can be a spectator, or you can be the athlete in the game. You can lead your life with intention, purpose, and a bold, determined vision. As the famous saying goes, "The only way to predict the future is to create it."[45] It's about taking charge of your life, following your instincts, and getting out of your own way.

When you live as the CEO of your existence, you're no longer a passive participant. You're making decisions, setting the course, and driving toward your goals with the same determination and focus that a visionary leader brings to their organization. And when obstacles arise, you don't let them stop you—you find a way around, over, or through them.

It's also about recognizing when someone doesn't align with your vision. If someone doesn't share your goals, values, or direction, it's okay to let them walk away. Not everyone is meant to be part of your journey, and that's perfectly fine. What's important is that you stay true to your vision and surround yourself with those who support and elevate it.

The Power of Visionary Thinking

Visionary thinking is at the heart of everything discussed in this book. It's the ability to imagine a future that is radically different and better than the present and live it today. It's the willingness to set goals others might consider impossible and to pursue them with relentless determination.

Throughout history, visionary thinkers have changed the world. From the Wright brothers to Elon Musk, these individuals dared to dream big and take bold actions to turn their dreams into reality. They didn't settle for the status quo or accept limitations imposed by society. Instead, they pushed the boundaries of what was possible and created new realities that transformed the world.

In your own life, visionary thinking is the key to achieving your most audacious goals. It's about seeing beyond the challenges of the present and focusing on the possibilities of the future. It's about believing in yourself and your vision, even when others doubt you. And it's about taking consistent, determined action to make that vision a reality.

As you move forward, continue to cultivate your visionary thinking. Surround yourself with people who support and inspire you and seek opportunities to challenge yourself and grow. The only limits are the ones you impose on yourself. The more you embrace your visionary thinking, the more you'll achieve and the greater impact you'll have on the world.

Taking Bold Action: Lead, Follow, or Get the Fuck Out of the Way

Bold action is the cornerstone of success. Having a vision or plan is not enough—you must act on it. Take daily steps that move you closer to your goals.

This is where the military mantra "Lead, follow, or get the fuck out of the way" comes into play. It's a call to action, a reminder that there's no room for hesitation or doubt in pursuing your dreams.

To lead your life effectively, you must first lead yourself. This means taking responsibility for your actions, decisions, and outcomes. It means setting clear goals, creating a plan to achieve them, and taking consistent action every day. It also means following your instincts—trusting that inner voice that knows what you're capable of and what you were put on this earth to do.

And then, of course, it means getting out of your own way. Too often, the biggest obstacles we face are the ones we create for ourselves. Fear, self-doubt, procrastination are all forms of self-sabotage that can derail even the best-laid plans. To succeed, recognize these obstacles for what they are and move past them. Be willing to step into your power and own your role as the CEO of your life.

Living boldly also means being unapologetic about your vision. Not everyone will understand or support your goals, and that's okay. You must be willing to say, "If we don't align, walk!" This isn't about arrogance but protecting your vision and staying true to your purpose. It's about knowing that not everyone is meant to be part of your journey. What's important is that you stay focused on your goals and surround yourself with people who believe in your vision as much as you do.

Building Your Legacy

Building my legacy has been about more than achieving my goals as an artist and entrepreneur. It's about creating something that will endure and inspire others to dream big and pursue their goals. It's about using my gifts and talents to make a positive impact on the world and leave it better than I found it for generations to come.

Part of building your legacy is being intentional about the choices you make and the actions you take. Every decision and every step contribute to the legacy you're building. It's important to stay true to your values and align your actions with the vision you have for your life and your impact on the world.

Building your legacy is about living with purpose, being mindful of your impact on others and the world, striving to be the best version of yourself, and using your gifts to make a difference. It's about leaving a lasting impact that will inspire and uplift others long after you're gone.

The Importance of Balance and Quality Time

In today's fast-paced world, it's easy to get caught up in the hustle and bustle of life. We're often told that more time equals more value and that the key to success is working harder and longer. But this mindset can harm our well-being and our ability to build a meaningful legacy.

Building my legacy has been about balancing and prioritizing quality time over quantity. I've learned that it's not about how *much* time you spend working but *how* you spend that time. It's about being intentional with your time and focusing on what truly matters.

In building your empire, you need to know when to push forward and when to take a step back and be present with the people you love. It's about understanding that quality time is more valuable than quantity and that being present in the moment is one of the greatest gifts you can give yourself and others.

While completing this book, there were two back-to-back nights when my youngest son, now about two and a half, was up in the middle of the night. I realized that being present with him, holding him until he fell back asleep, was more important than pushing through exhaustion to work. If you, too, are building your empire, you need to know when to go and when to slow. I'm learning every day that being still isn't bad when it comes to being present and experiencing life in the moment; it's a gift.

Moving Forward with Confidence

You have the power to achieve anything you set your mind to. You can overcome any obstacle, push through any challenge, and build a legacy that will inspire and uplift others.

Your journey won't always be easy, and there will be times when you face doubt, fear, and uncertainty. But in those moments, remember that you can achieve great things. You have the power to create the life you want and to make a positive impact on the world.

As you move forward, continue to cultivate your visionary thinking, take consistent action, and stay true to your values. Surround yourself with people who support and inspire you, and never stop striving to be the best version of yourself.

Remember, your legacy is not just about what you achieve in your lifetime; it's about the impact you leave on the world and the lives you touch. So go out there and build your legacy, one step at a time. The world is waiting for you.

Conclusion: The Journey Continues

Thank you for joining me on this journey. It's been an honor to share my story, my experiences, and the lessons I've learned along the way. My hope is that this book has inspired you to dream big, take bold actions, and build a legacy that will make a difference in the world.

So go out there and make your wildest dreams a reality. The world is waiting for you to achieve your DUMB goals!

REFERENCES

1   Winfrey, Oprah. 2011. Master Class. Oprah Winfrey Network.

2   Hill, Napolean. (1937). Think and Grow Rich.

3   Kennedy, John F. "We Choose to Go to the Moon." Speech, Rice University, Houston, TX, September 12, 1962

4   Walsch, N. D. (2010). When Everything Changes, Change Everything: In a Time of Turmoil, A Pathway to Peace. Hay House, Inc.

5   Robbins, Tony. Money: Master the Game. Simon & Schuster, 2014

6   Friedman, Meyer, and Ray Rosenman. Type A Behavior and Your Heart. Knopf, 1959

7   Kotler, Philip. Marketing Management. 15th ed., Pearson, 2016.

8   Smith, John, and Emily Johnson. 2023. "The Role of Daily Goals in Long-Term Success." Journal of Applied Psychology 108, no. 3: 450-460

9   Sonnentag, S., & Frese, M. (2002). Performance concepts and performance theory. Journal of Applied Psychology, 87(3), 498-506. Retrieved September 17, 2024 from https://doi.org/10.1037/0021-9010.87.3.498.

10 Smith, Laura, and James Thompson. 2022. "The Impact of Celebrating Small Wins on Long-Term

Motivation and Goal Achievement." The European Journal of Social Psychology 53, no. 4: 315-330.

11   Johnson, Sarah, and Michael Lee. 2021. "The Power of Visualization in Goal Achievement: A Study on Task Performance." University of California, Los Angeles.

12   Clance, Pauline R., and Suzanne A. Imes. 1978. "The Impostor Phenomenon in High Achieving Women: Dynamics and Therapeutic Intervention."

13   Kets de Vries, Manfred F.R. 2005. "The Dangers of Feeling Like a Fake." Harvard Business Review.

14   Dweck, Carol S. 2006. Mindset: The New Psychology of Success. New York: Random House.

15   Beck, Aaron T. 1976. Cognitive Therapy and the Emotional Disorders. New York: International Universities Press.

16   Ellis, Albert, and Robert A. Harper. 1975. A New Guide to Rational Living. Englewood Cliffs, NJ: Prentice-Hall.

17   Brown, Brené. 2010. The Gifts of Imperfection: Let Go of Who You Think You're Supposed to Be and Embrace Who You Are. Hazelden Publishing.

18   Cloud, Henry, and John Townsend. 1992. Boundaries: When to Say Yes, How to Say No to Take Control of Your Life. Zondervan.

19   Covey, Stephen R. 1989. The 7 Habits of Highly Effective People: Powerful Lessons in Personal Change. New York: Free Press.

20   Burns, David D. 1980. Feeling Good: The New Mood Therapy. New York: HarperCollins.

21 Seligman, Martin E.P. 1975. Helplessness: On Depression, Development, and Death. San Francisco: W.H. Freeman.

22 American Psychological Association. "Children's Cognitive Development." American Psychological Association, 2021. https://www.apa.org

23 Doidge, Norman. The Brain That Changes Itself: Stories of Personal Triumph from the Frontiers of Brain Science. Viking Penguin, 2007.

24 See Guang Yue and Cole, 1992.

25 Dweck, Carol S. (2006). Mindset: The New Psychology of Success. Random House.

26 Locke, E. A., & Latham, G. P. (2002). Building a practically useful theory of goal setting and task motivation: A 35-year odyssey. American Psychologist, 57(9), 705-717.

27 Taylor, S. E. (1995). Health psychology: The science and the field. American Psychologist, 50(4), 276-281.

28 Fredrickson, B. L. (2001). The role of positive emotions in positive psychology: The broaden-and-build theory of positive emotions. American Psychologist, 56(3), 218-226

29 Dweck, C. S. (2006). Mindset: The New Psychology of Success. Random House.

30 Gollwitzer, P. M. (1999). Implementation intentions: Strong effects of simple plans. American Psychologist, 54(7), 493-503.

31 Matthews, G. (2015). The Effectiveness of Written Goals. Dominican University of California.

32 Robbins, T. (2001). Awaken the Giant Within: How to Take Immediate Control of Your Mental, Emotional, Physical and Financial Destiny! Free Press.

33 Harvey, S. (2016). Jump: Take the Leap of Faith to Achieve Your Life of Abundance. Amista

34 Guang Yue, K. M., & Cole, K. J. (1992). Strength increases from the motor program: Comparison of training with maximal voluntary and imagined muscle contractions. Journal of Neurophysiology, 67(5), 1114-1123.

35 Ziglar, Z. (2007). Zig Ziglar's Life Lifters: Moments of Inspiration for Living Life Better. B&H Publishing Group.

36 Pareto, Vilfredo. 1935. The Mind and Society. Dover Publications.

37 Koch, Richard. The 80/20 Principle: The Secret to Achieving More with Less. Crown Business, 1999.

38 U.S. Air Force Core Values. "Excellence in All We Do." U.S. Air Force, 2023. www.airforce.com.

39 Koch, Richard. The 80/20 Principle: The Secret to Achieving More with Less. Crown Business, 1999.

40 Ellis, Albert. Reason and Emotion in Psychotherapy. Lyle Stuart, 1962.

41 Weick, K. E. (1984). Small Wins: Redefining the Scale of Social Problems. American Psychologist, 39(1), 40-49.

42 Tracy, Brian. Eat That Frog!: 21 Great Ways to Stop Procrastinating and Get More Done in Less Time. Berrett-Koehler Publishers, 2001.

43   Beck, J. S. (2011). Cognitive Behavior Therapy: Basics and Beyond. Guilford Press.

44   NASA. "Creativity and Innovation in Engineering: NASA's 1960s Experiments." NASA Historical Archives, 1968.

45   Drucker, P. F. (1954). The Practice of Management. Harper & Row

ABOUT JULIE JAMISON

Julie Jamison is a visionary entrepreneur, fine art photographer, and dynamic leader dedicated to the creative arts.

As the Founder and CEO of GATE 28 & J. Rose Scrolls Galleries, Julie established herself in the luxury fine art photography space, creating exclusively one of one fine art photography pieces that captivate collectors and designers. Her work merges traditional artistry with cutting-edge AI techniques, producing masterpieces that are not only visually stunning but also stand as long-term investments.

Julie has served nearly 13 years, both active duty as a Nuclear Missile Operator and continues to serve as an Aircraft Maintenance Officer in the U.S. Air Force Reserve. Her military background has been instrumental in shaping her approach to business and art.

Her corporate experience, including leadership roles in quality assurance and operations, adds a strategic edge to her creative endeavors. She's led teams of professionals, implemented process improvements, and ensured compliance with rigorous standards across multiple sectors. This blend of precision, creativity, and business acumen has been key to her success as an artist and an entrepreneur.

She teaches and mentors at the collegiate level, preparing young adults to serve as military officers, covering topics ranging from leadership basics and team building to giving and receiving feedback.

Julie and her husband, Joe, live in Ohio with their four children.

Contact Julie at www.thejuliejamison.com

Julie at the Akron Art
Museum

Kentucky Derby themed
Fundraiser

Julie photographing at the Louvre

4 - PINK & WHITE ROSES - J. ROSE
SCROLLS - MARCH 2024
by Julie Jamison

Enjoying Paris near the PAD

Pink & White Roses - SOLD

If you've enjoyed this book, we ask you to consider leaving a review on Amazon, Barnes & Noble, Audible, and Goodreads. It does not need to be long, but reviews really help the online platforms find new readers for books. If you have friends or family who you think would enjoy this book, please recommend it to them. Word of mouth remains the best marketing any author can hope for.